INSIGHT

C000143940

Beijing

Discovery
CHANNEL

APA PUBLICATIONS L

Part of the Langenscheidt Publishing Group

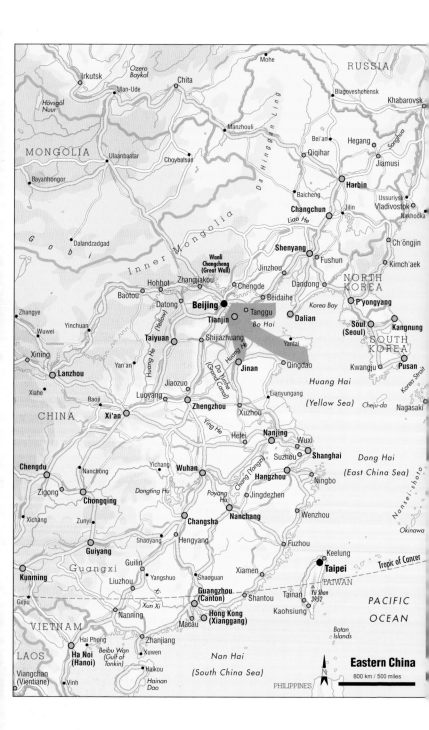

Eastern China

800 km / 500 miles

introduction

Welcome

This guidebook combines the interests and enthusiasms of two of the world's best-known information providers: Insight Guides, who have set the standard for visual travel guides since 1970, and Discovery Channel, the world's premier source of non-fiction television programming. Its aim is to bring you the best of Beijing and its environs in a series of tailor-made itineraries devised by Insight's Beijing correspondent, Kari Huus.

Beijing is all about grandiosity – the Great Wall, the Forbidden City, Tiananmen Square and the Temple of Heaven. It is, after all, the capital for one-fifth of the world's population. Throughout the centuries, every ruler has moulded the city in his own image, creating layer upon layer of architectural statements spanning centuries. But Beijing is also a series of villages that creep between and sprawl beyond the halls of power. In the various *hutong* (alleyways) of the city, life comprises myriad wonderful little traditions – like raising crickets and flying kites. To help you cover these fascinating contrasts, the author has put together 10 itineraries that cover Beijing and its surroundings. The full-day day itineraries include all the major highlights while the shorter tours take in a variety of historical sites, temples, parks, markets and myriad *hutong*.

There are also three excursions to places further afield: the famous Great Wall and Ming Tombs; Bedaihe beach, where China's top brass hobnob; and Chengde, an old imperial summer retreat. The carefully-devised itineraries in this book anticipate the vagaries of travel in China and offer advice on how to cope. Chapters on shopping, eating out and nightlife, and a useful practical information section on travel essentials complete this reader-friendly guide.

Kari Huus has seen the many faces of Beijing in her four years in the city, as a former reporter for *Newsweek* magazine and an avid explorer of the city's back streets. She arrived in the aftermath of the 1989 Tiananmen Square protests and was present throughout its dramatic wave of economic reform. 'It feels like I've been living in several different places at the same time. The mood and the landscape of the city keep changing,' she says, 'depending on your vantage point.' A fluent speaker of Mandarin, Huus knows people as diverse as communist officials, playwrights and bicycle repairmen. She brings a keen insight and enthusiasm to this book, filled with details that bring this historically rich and quirky capital to life.

6   **contents**

EXCURSIONS

Three excursions, both day and overnight, to places within easy reach of Beijing.

LEISURE ACTIVITIES

CALENDAR OF EVENTS

PRACTICAL INFORMATION

MAPS

CREDITS AND INDEX

Pages 2/3: the Summer Palace
Pages 8/9: Nine Dragon Screen, Beihai Park

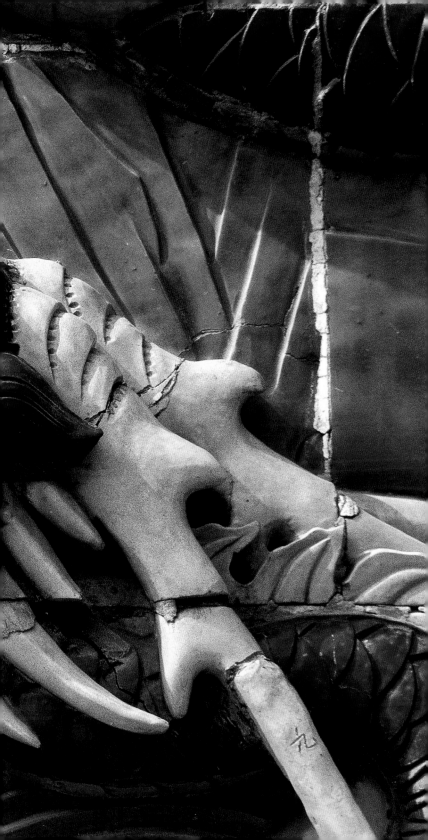

History
&Culture

T he well-worn image of Chairman Mao standing on Tiananmen Gate (Gate of Heavenly Peace) and proclaiming the founding of the People's Republic of China, is symbolic of Beijing's emergence as the modern capital of this vast country. Throughout China's history the city's rise has been violent and uncertain. Only after many cycles of destruction and reconstruction did the former garrison town become the political and cultural centre of the Middle Kingdom.

Frontier Days

The discovery of the skull of the Peking Man near Beijing in 1929 proved that prehistoric humans settled here more than 500,000 years ago. Yet little more is known until about 5,000 years ago, by which time neolithic agricultural villages had been established within the area of the modern city. The recorded history of the city begins around 1000BC, when it was a trading town called Ji. Its strategic location, on the border of the agricultural plains to the south and the open steppes to the north, made it a garrison town which changed hands repeatedly between the warring kingdoms of the north.

Qin Shi Huangdi, the first emperor of the Qin dynasty, unified China in 221BC, making Ji a part of one of the world's largest empires. He was obsessed with protecting China's northern frontier, and connected walls built by previous kingdoms to form the Great Wall. The massive project was continued by successive rulers using conscript labour, but Ji was often raided by northern tribes. During the Liao dynasty (AD 916–1125), the city was renamed Yanjing and in the 12th century was called Zhongdu (Central Capital). The city underwent another transformation when 'barbarian' conquerors from the north, the Mongols who founded the Yuan dynasty in the 13th century, proclaimed Zhongdu the capital of the new dynasty.

Mongol Conquest and Rule

When Genghis Khan's armies stormed Beijing in 1215, the month-long invasion was the most brutal yet. The court's treasures were looted and the city was razed. But it was from these ashes that arose one of the world's greatest capitals. By 1279, Genghis Khan's grandson, Kublai Khan, ruled not only all of China but also much of the Eurasian land mass, from parts of Vietnam and Burma to the Baltic Sea. But, like many before him and since, Kublai Khan was as much conquered by Chinese culture as he was the conqueror of its territory. He was fascinated by Buddhism and China's advanced knowledge of astronomy and agriculture.

Left: terracotta warriors, Xi'an, from the Qin dynasty
Right: print of Qin Emperor Qin Shi Huangdi

Kublai Khan's capital, then known as Dadu (Great Capital) in Chinese and Khan Balik (City of the Khan) in Mongolian, was built on the present site of Beijing. Because of a lack of educated Mongol officials, his administrators were mostly Chinese; his capital a copy of traditional Chinese capitals.

Marco Polo, who allegedly served at the court of the Khan for 17 years (although it has been argued that the Italian merchant fabricated his voyage), marvelled at the chessboard precision of the city's layout, and its broad, straight streets lined with fine courtyard homes and inns. Hostels in the suburbs, and some 20,000 prostitutes, served merchants from all over the world. In the city centre, on the site of today's Beihai Park, stood Kublai Khan's palace surrounded by a 6½-km (4-mile) wall.

The Mongols improved roads and canals, leading to an increase in both regional and international trade. By the end of Kublai Khan's reign in 1293, the Tonghua Canal had been completed, linking the capital with the Grand Canal. Dadu's population had grown to around 500,000.

Like their counterparts in previous dynasties, later Yuan officials and civil servants became increasingly corrupt and inept. The Mongols exported much of China's wealth to other parts of their kingdom, and starvation was widespread. Heavy taxes were levied on citizens who were not of Mongol descent. No longer faced with a shortage of educated personnel, the Mongol rulers excluded Chinese from government posts, choosing Mongols or foreigners instead. The Chinese had become third-class citizens in their own country, behind the Mongols and their central Asian allies. Not surprisingly, in 1368, an army of impoverished Chinese peasants overthrew the Yuan dynasty and brought about the end of Mongol rule in China.

The Ming Dynasty

With the founding of the Ming dynasty (1368–1644), the Chinese were again masters of a unified China. The new rulers moved their capital to Nanjing, in the heart of a rich agricultural region to the south. But, with an eye to expand China's territory northward, Ming Emperor Yongle soon moved the capital back to its previous location, naming it Beijing (Northern Capital).

Emperor Yongle's reign (1403–25) was the cultural pinnacle of imperial Beijing, particularly in architecture. The Forbidden City (sometimes known as the Imperial Palace), was constructed under Yongle and has remained symbolic of Beijing's pre-eminence ever since. Tiananmen Gate, now adorned with Mao's portrait, is also a legacy of that period. So is another of the city's most striking structures, the Temple of Heaven (Tiantan), where the emperor communed with the gods twice yearly. Yongle also rebuilt Kublai Khan's city walls around the imperial city and added another rectangle encompassing the Temple of Heaven in the south.

Above: Kublai Khan ruled from 1271 until 1294
Right: an early view of the Forbidden City

Throughout the Ming dynasty, emperors mobilised huge armies of labourers to fortify the Great Wall. Much of it was rebuilt, and many new towers and some whole sections were added, especially near Beijing. More than 200 years of continuous construction resulted in a 3,000-km (1,900-mile) wall.

Soon after Emperor Yongle's death, however, China closed itself to the outside world and forbade its people to emigrate or explore foreign lands. Foreigners were, by and large, despised for their barbarian ways. The Chinese also rejected Western science, which had just begun to revolutionise the outside world. This paranoia and insecurity led to a slowdown of China's development in areas such as astronomy and navigation, in which it had once been a world leader.

Each successive emperor became increasingly enmeshed in elaborate palace ceremonies and isolated from the outside world. Palace eunuchs became corrupt and powerful, siphoning riches from the palace and extracting heavy taxes from the poor. They controlled information to the emperor so that news of peasant rebellions did not always reach him. Not surprisingly, another peasant uprising toppled the Ming dynasty in 1644 and paved the way for an invasion from the northeast, by the Manchus, 43 days later.

The Qing Dynasty

Unlike the invaders before them, the Manchus who founded the Qing dynasty (1644–1911) did not destroy the city they occupied. Prolific builders and renovators, the Qing rulers built lavish palaces, mixing the styles of past dynasties, often with gaudy results. Many of the 800 or so pavilions, palaces and temples built by the Ming were preserved into the 20th century. Most of the relics in Beijing date from the 600 years of Ming and Qing rule.

The Qing emperors tried to grapple with the problems that had toppled the Ming. They maintained the examination system for choosing officials, slashed the number of eunuchs to minimise court intrigue and tried to reform the tax system. By far the most colourful character was Qianlong (1736–99), the longest reigning Chinese emperor. He was a despot who ruthlessly suppressed intellectuals suspected of disloyalty. But he loved the arts and was respon-

sible for some of the city's more flamboyant architectural details. The exquisite arts collection in the Forbidden City is due mainly to Qianlong's intense passion for the arts.

The drive for expansion that began with the Ming dynasty's Yongle carried on into the Qing dynasty and became the main focus of their 267-year reign. Under Emperor Qianlong, Chinese territory expanded dramatically northwards and westwards. By the end of the 19th century, Beijing ruled over four times as much territory as it had during the Ming dynasty.

End of Empire

While China was expanding in the 18th and 19th centuries, Western colonial powers were changing the face of the globe. Beijing became increasingly suspicious of the outside world. Foreign trade was limited to Guangzhou (Canton) and frustrated by complex regulations. The British, who were keen to acquire better access to the Chinese market, sent a high-level delegation in 1793 to the Chinese port of Tianjin, aboard a warship loaded with expensive gifts and state-of-the-art technology. But Emperor Qianlong rebuffed the British with an edict to King George III, saying that China did not need to trade with Britain because she 'already possessed everything a civilised people could ever want'. Britain's request to set up a consulate in Beijing was also rejected.

But Britain would not take no for an answer. Backed by military force, foreign traders pressed shipments of opium on the Chinese market to offset Britain's growing trade deficit. The First Opium War of 1839–42 forced the palace to allow foreign governments extra-territoriality in an area just outside the palace gates. By the end of the Second Opium War in 1860, the emperor had fled to Chengde while Western troops destroyed a large swathe of the city, including the old Summer Palace. The rulers' impotence infuriated the Chinese; secret societies sprang up and small-scale rebellions became common.

In the final days of the Qing dynasty, the palace was a fortress against the reality of China's decay and the stage where the last court tragedy was acted out. The emperor's favourite concubine, Empress Cixi, rose to eminence after a power struggle in the palace in 1861. She dominated and terrorised the court, but could not hold the crumbling kingdom together.

In 1900, a secret society called the Boxers laid siege to the Foreign Legation Quarter for 50 days and Empress Cixi was forced to flee. Before her death in 1908, she installed three-year-old Pu Yi on the throne, who was to be the last of China's emperors. His story is told in the 1988 movie, *The Last Emperor*.

Above: Pu Yi as a young child

The Republican Era

In 1911, a revolution led by Dr Sun Yat-sen attempted to launch China into the modern world and restore the country to its people. It ended imperial rule, but the old problems of feuding warlords, poverty, factionalism and foreign invasion continued for another 30 years.

At the end of World War I, Western powers continued to carve up China for themselves. The Treaty of Versailles ceded Chinese territory to the Japanese, humiliating China. The reaction to this marked a turning point in the Chinese people's psyche: students and intellectuals around the country took to the streets in what came to be known as the May Fourth Movement of 1919, demanding independence and territorial integrity.

In 1927, the Nationalist Party (Kuomintang), under Chiang Kai-shek, tried to unify China again by force. On 10 October 1928, it formally founded the Republic of China (ROC) with its capital in Nanjing. In the countryside, the Chinese Communist Party (CCP), founded in Shanghai in 1921 and led by the young Mao Zedong, waged a guerrilla war against the new government. But the Japanese occupation of China soon forced the Nationalists and the Communists to form an uneasy alliance that lasted until the end of World War II. In the bitter civil war that followed, the Communists were victorious and Chiang Kai-shek and two million other Nationalists fled to Taiwan.

Communist China

In true imperial style, Mao Zedong declared the founding of the People's Republic of China (PRC) from Tiananmen Gate on 1 October 1949, restoring Beijing as the capital. The new leaders took to their task with zeal, redistributing land to the peasants, and undertaking massive industrialisation projects. In Beijing, slums were razed, and new Soviet-style factories, offices, apartment blocks and universities built. In 1957, most of the city walls, hundreds of temples and historical sites were demolished as 12,000 'volunteers' worked at breakneck speed to complete Tiananmen Square and the gargantuan buildings surrounding it in time for the PRC's 10th anniversary.

But the euphoria was followed by a series of political campaigns that left deep scars on the whole nation. The Anti-Rightist Movement of 1957 targeted intellectuals, capitalists and other 'class enemies'. Hot on its heels was the Great Leap Forward (1958–60), a disastrous attempt at overnight modernisation that led to mass starvation in the countryside.

However, the most devastating mass movement was the Cultural Revolution (1966–76). Millions of young zealots were mobilised to wage war on feudal and bourgeois culture. Many people were denounced as traitors or class enemies and lost their jobs, possessions, liberty and often their lives. Young people and educated adults from Beijing and other

Right: Mao Zedong proclaims the founding of the People's Republic of China, 1949

urban areas were also sent to the countryside to 'learn from the peasants'. Most had no idea when or if they would be allowed to return. Fear and chaos reigned until Mao's death in September 1976. In the last years of his life, the notorious Gang of Four, led by Mao's wife, Jiang Qing, used the movement to seize power. The death of Premier Zhou Enlai in January 1976, a moderating force in the government, sparked mass mourning in Beijing that turned into an outcry for change. Later that year, the Gang of Four were arrested and tried. The two perceived leaders of the group – Jiang Qing and Zhang Chunqiao – were given suspended death sentences and the remaining two members received lengthy prison terms.

Reform Years

After Mao's death, Beijing struggled to modernise. Communist ideology was gradually discarded for pragmatic economic reform under Deng Xiaoping's leadership in the years following 1978. China began to open up and there was more contact with foreigners. The rigid bureaucracy gave way, at least in the economic sphere, to a more freewheeling society.

But these policies involved a delicate balancing act, more evident in Beijing than elsewhere. In 1979, the Democracy Wall movement brought

millions onto the streets, calling for greater political freedom. In 1986, a democratic movement in the central Chinese city of Hefei sparked protests in Beijing and Shanghai. Both events, led by students and intellectuals, were followed by greater repression of the press, arts and political reformers. In 1989, millions of students and workers marched to Tiananmen Square to protest against corruption and appeal for political reform.

When the military moved in to quell the protests on 4 June, several hundred demonstrators were killed. Political reform had been ruled out and remains a distant, half-forgotten dream. The idea of the socialist market economy, accredited to Deng, became the core of party policy; and it remained the central mainstay of the reform years through the Jiang Zemin years and is set to continue under President Jiang's successor-in-waiting, Hu Jintao. Economic development remains vital to the Communist party's continuation; any major economic setback could spark dissent and give free rein to nationwide disillusionment, as has happened so often in China's history.

The historic, but controversial, decision to award Beijing the 2008 Olympic Games is set to spur the city to yet more growth and investment in the coming years. It is hoped that this, in turn, will lead to improvements in human rights and political stability in China.

Above: flags flying in Tianamen Square

HISTORY HIGHLIGHTS

1030–221BC: The city of Ji develops on the site of Beijing.

221–207BC: Emperor Qin Shi Huangdi unifies China and begins Great Wall.

200BC–AD1200: Beijing becomes a strategic garrison town between warring kingdoms.

1215: Mongols led by Genghis Khan overrun Beijing.

1260: Kublai Khan founds the Mongol (Yuan) dynasty.

1271: Kublai Khan establishes the capital of Dadu (Khan Balik) at Beijing. Marco Polo visits China, and serves at the court of the Khan for 17 years.

1368–1644 The Ming dynasty.

1400s: Forbidden City and most of the existing Great Wall built.

1644–1911: Qing (Manchu) dynasty is established.

1839–42: The First Opium War.

1860: The Second Opium War.

1861–1908: Empress Cixi holds power.

1900: Boxer Rebellion lays siege to the Foreign Legation Quarter.

1911: Revolution headed by Sun Yat-sen ends imperial rule.

1919: Treaty of Versailles cedes territory to Japan and sparks May Fourth Movement for democracy and sovereignty.

1921: The Chinese Communist Party is founded in Shanghai.

1928: The Nationalist government establishes its capital in Nanjing.

1935: Communists embark on the Long March to escape Nationalist forces.

1937: The Marco Polo Bridge incident precedes a full-scale invasion by the Japanese, who occupy much of China until the end of World War II.

1949: Mao Zedong declares the founding of the People's Republic of China. Beijing becomes the capital.

1957–59: Tiananmen Square and surrounding monoliths built. Most of the city wall is demolished.

1957: The Anti-Rightist Movement singles out 300,000 intellectuals for criticism, punishment or imprisonment.

1958: Mao launches the disastrous Great Leap Forward.

1959–62: Famine claims 20 million.

1960: Beijing and Moscow split, beginning two decades of Cold War.

1966–76: Cultural Revolution leads to widespread persecution, chaos and near economic collapse.

1972: President Nixon visits Beijing, first official contact between US and PRC.

1976: Premier Zhou Enlai and Chairman Mao die. Gang of Four arrested.

1978: Premier Deng Xiaoping launches economic reforms.

1979: Democracy Wall Movement is quashed.

1980: Gang of Four tried on nationwide television. Reforms are effected.

1989: Tiananmen Square democracy demonstration is crushed by military.

1992: Japanese Emperor Akihito visits China. Deng Xiaoping tours South.

1993: China's parliament officially endorses market economy and begins a series of structural reforms to its finanical, currency and taxation systems.

1997: Deng Xiaoping dies. Hong Kong returns to China. President Jiang Zemin consolidates power.

1998: President Clinton visits China. China suffers worst flood in a century.

1999: China celebrates 50th anniversary of its founding. Macau returns to China. Policy established to speed up the development of western China.

2001: Beijing is chosen as host city for the 2008 Olympic Games; China joins the WTO.

2003: Hu Jintao replaces Jiang Zemin as president; Wen Jiabao replaces Zhu Rongji as Premier.

2004: Hu Jintao takes over from Jiang Zemin as Head of Military.

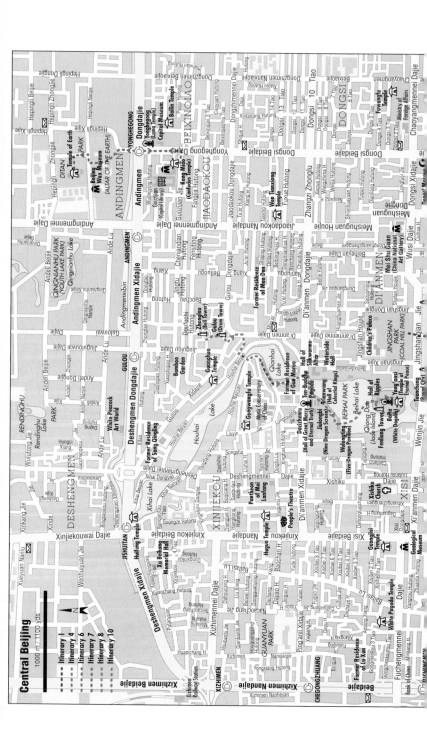

Central Beijing

1000 m/1100 yds

Itinerary 1
Itinerary 4
Itinerary 6
Itinerary 7
Itinerary 8
Itinerary 10

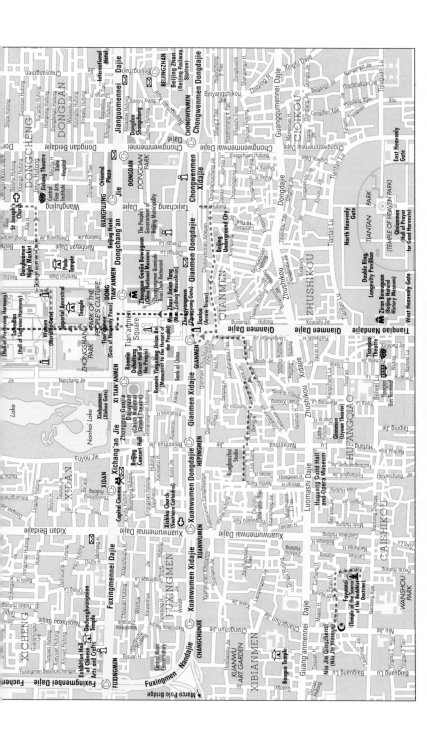

Beijing & Environs

Beijing is the capital and political nerve centre of China, but it's far from the geographical centre. Located on the northern plain 180km (112 miles) from the ocean, it suffers bitter winters and blistering summers. The good news is that, despite being home to more than 14 million people, it is less congested than most other large Chinese cities.

Beijing municipality covers 16,808sq km (6,488sq miles), so sightseeing entails covering a lot of ground. The city is laid out on a grid, with Dongchang'an Jie (Avenue of Eternal Peace) dividing the city into the northern and southern sections. Street names change according to their relationship to the gates of the former city wall. Dongchang'an Jie, for example, turns into Fuxingmennei meaning 'inside Fuxing Gate' to the west and Fuxingmenwai or 'outside Fuxing Gate' further west. Four ring roads loop around the city, and a fifth is being constructed.

Taxis and bicycles are the best forms of transport in Beijing. Taxis are numerous and reasonably priced. The modest subway is being extended and is useful for getting to the general vicinity of your destination. Bicycles are a good way to see the city and can be rented at hotels across the city, or around Qianhou Hai.

Exploring the City

The following 10 itineraries take in Beijing's world-famous sights, starting with Tiananmen Square and the Forbidden City (Imperial Palace). The first two itineraries take a full day each. Itineraries 3 to 8 are shorter, mostly taking a half-day to complete. Itineraries 9 and 10 are evening tours.

The itineraries are punctuated with temples, parks and museums, but also lead you through the city's maze of alleyways (*hutong*) to some interesting neighbourhoods and markets. By big city standards, Beijing is remarkably safe, friendly and inexpensive, so take the listed suggestions as jump-off points for your own explorations. Any free time you have will not be wasted – simply walk the city's streets and turn down any *hutong* you happen to come across. Beijing is a city of walls; only exploring beyond them and into the various *hutong* can you see the traditional life of Beijingers. Each and every corner holds the possibility of a unique experience.

There are also three longer excursions out of the city, which will take in the Great Wall of China and Ming Tombs, the Bedaihe beach resort and the great mountain retreat of the Qing emperors, Chengde.

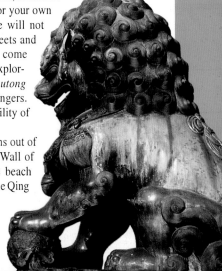

Left: the Forbidden City
Right: a bronze lion stands guard

1. TIANANMEN SQUARE, FORBIDDEN CITY AND JINGSHAN PARK *(see maps, pages 23 and 24)*

A front door to back door trek through the imperial heart of the city, leading through Tiananmen Square, the Forbidden City and the gardens of Jingshan Park. This is a full day tour.

Take the subway to the Qianmen stop. You can also reach Tiananmen by taking the subway to both Xi Tiananmen and Dong Tiananmen stops.

A first day of exploring Beijing starts logically enough at **Qianmen** (Front Gate). This tower (open daily 8am–4pm; entrance fee) is the largest of nine similar gates in the wall that used to embrace the Inner City, which has at its centre the Imperial Palace or Forbidden City. Qianmen, built in 1419, was initially used solely for the emperor's annual visits to the Temple of Heaven, where, after three days of fasting, he would pray for a good harvest. Residents outside the gate were forbidden to glimpse upon the procession, and had to keep their doors and windows sealed. Destroyed during the Boxer Rebellion of 1900, the gate was rebuilt in 1905. The front gate provides a great vantage point for studying the layout of old Beijing.

The north section of Qianmen, across the street, is **Zhengyangmen** ('Facing the Sun Gate'; main entrance), while Qianmen's southern gate is **Jianlou** (Arrow Tower), built in 1439 to serve as a watchtower. The Outer City, which was also enclosed by a high wall, extends southward. The bustling, narrow streets to the south form the lively Dazhalan shopping district *(see Itinerary 5)*, which at the end of the 19th century teemed with decadent pleasures for off-duty officials. Further south is the Temple of Heaven *(see Itinerary 3)*.

The north side of Qianmen overlooks **Tiananmen Square**, in the middle of which stands an obelisk. To the left stands the Great Hall of the People and to the right the China National Museum; in the centre of the square is the Mao Zedong Mausoleum.

At the far end of the square, across Dongchang'an Jie, is Tiananmen Gate, or the Gate of Heavenly Peace, leading the way to the Forbidden City, now officially known as the Palace Museum (Gugong). To the immediate west of Tiananmen Gate is the entrance to Zhongshan (Sun Yat-sen) Park, dedicated to the early Nationalist leader. The park used to be part of the Forbidden City, as did Zhongnanhai, a little further west, where China's top leaders now live. To the northwest you will see the white dagoba in Beihai Park, once part of the imperial gardens.

Views of the Past

Before leaving Qianmen, visit the photo exhibition inside. There are wonderful views of Beijing at the turn of the century, from cricket fighting to camel caravans arriving at the city gate. Next, join the queue to pay your respects at the **Mao Zedong Mausoleum** (Mao Zhuxi Jinian Tang;

Left: Tiananmen guard
Top right: the Great Hall of the People

Tues–Sun 8–11.30am, Wed–Fri 2–4pm; free), completed in 1977, a year after his death. Even today, when the little red book of Mao quotations is long past its sell-by date, people from all over China visit his mausoleum. As you file past the Great Helmsman – one of the four Grand Old Men of Marxism-Leninism who are lying in state – you are likely to ponder the rumours of body-doubles, nightly deep-freezes and parts falling off the Chairman. But also be aware of the reverence paid by those around you. Entrance is free, but you must leave your bag at the door. Though the queue looks daunting, visitors are hustled through quickly. Just outside the mausoleum, you get a graphic picture of how socialism is fast becoming

mere consumer kitsch, as people are ushered through a small bazaar selling Chairman Mao busts, bags, badges and musical lighters playing *The East is Red*.

Memorials and Museums

The 37m (121ft) obelisk that you saw earlier in the centre of Tiananmen Square is called the **Monument to the People's Heroes** (Renmin Yingxiong Jinian Bei), dedicated in 1958 to those who died for the country. The bas relief on the pedestal portrays the struggle from the First Opium War

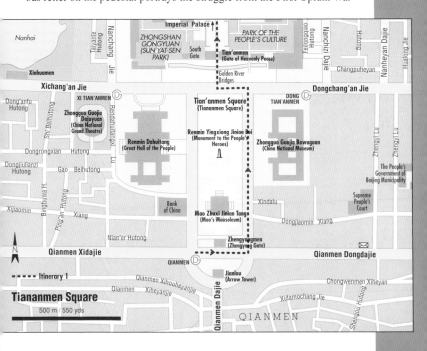

Tiananmen Square
500 m / 550 yds

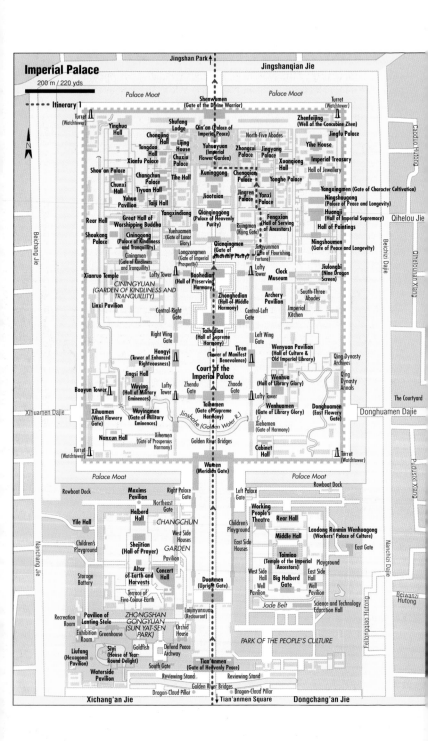

Right: Tiananmen Gate, with Mao's portrait

(1839–42) to the founding of the PRC in 1949. Start on the east side and move clockwise to see it chronologically.

Next, visit the **Great Hall of the People** (Renmin Dahuitang; open daily 8.30am–3pm except during meetings; entrance fee), officially opened in 1959, where China's parliament, the National People's Congress, meets and other important conferences and diplomatic meetings take place. One room of the hall is dedicated to each of China's 32 provinces and regions. If you enjoy political history, cross the square to the imposing Stalinist-style **China National Museum** (Zhongguo Guojia Bowuguan; open daily 9am–4pm; entrance fee), comprising the former **Museum of the Chinese Revolution and Museum of Chinese History**, which were combined in February 2003. The Museum of Chinese Revolution features photographs, paintings, documents and relics representing the key events and personalities that brought communism to China. The Museum of Chinese History covers the entire history of China, and has many ancient and unique cultural relics. At the time of press, however, much of the collection in the museums has been packed up in preparation for an early-2005 expansion.

The Great Meeting Place

Relax for a while in **Tiananmen Square**. In Ming and Qing times two rows of ministry offices stood on this site. When the emperor wanted to hand down an edict, he would pass with great fanfare to deliver it to the Ministry of Rites, where it was recopied and distributed throughout the empire. Many buildings were demolished to make Tiananmen larger than any other public square, including Moscow's Red Square. The area has been the venue for anti-government demonstrations, mass rallies and parades both before and since the building of the square. Now it's a convenient place for locals to meet and show off kite-flying, soccer or photography skills. Tiananmen Square has been prettified as part of efforts to beautify the city for the 2008 Olympics. A daily flag-raising and lowering ceremony is performed by PLA soldiers in the north of the square at sunrise and sunset.

beijing & environs

For lunch, check out the Qianmen neighbourhood, just south of the square, or Wangfujing, a short walk or pedicab ride east.

After lunch, return to the **Tiananmen Gate** (Gate of Heavenly Peace), to enter **Forbidden City** where China's revolutionary and feudal legacies converge. The gate, built in 1417 and restored in 1651, is now adorned with Mao's portrait and the slogans: 'Long live the People's Republic of China' and 'Long live the great union of the peoples of the world'. It was here that Mao announced the founding of the People's Republic of China (PRC) before a crowd of 300,000 in 1949.

The Forbidden City

From Tiananmen Gate, a long approach takes you through a second gate before reaching the **Forbidden City** (open daily 8.30am–4.30pm; entrance fee). Whether referred to by its official Chinese name of **Palace Museum** (Gugong) or its more well-known Western sobriquet, the Forbidden City, this is a sight you should not miss. A useful and informative audio guide, available in eight languages, can be rented for a guided tour of the palace's main buildings. Visitors can move at their own pace between signposted and numbered points. Actor Roger Moore reads the English commentary. To collect an audio guide, enter the Forbidden City through glass doors to the right of the main entrance. When restoration work on Emperor Qianlong's retirement quarters is completed, an even more jaw-dropping sight awaits: an East-meets-West artistic Nirvana.

Behind walls more than 10m (30ft) high, and within the 50m (160ft) moat, life in the palace was dictated by complex rules and rituals. Entrance was denied to ordinary people, but the gigantic gateway leads today's tourists to a fascinating display of Chinese cultural history in what is probably the best-preserved site of classical Chinese architecture.

In 1421, after 17 years of construction, the Ming Emperor Yongle moved into the palace. Up to the founding of the republic in 1911 – a period covering the reign of 24 emperors from the Ming dynasty until the last emperor, Puyi – the palace was the imperial residence and centre of the

Middle Kingdom. It has 9,000 rooms in which an estimated 8,000 to 10,000 people lived, including 3,000 eunuchs, as well as maids and concubines, all within an area of 70 hectares (180 acres).

The entire site can be divided into two large areas: **Waichao**, the Outer Court, in the south, and in the rear, **Neiting**, the Inner Residence. Through the middle of the site runs the imperial walkway, which is decorated with finely carved stone dragon and phoenix bas-reliefs, representing the emperor and the empress.

Among the details to look out for are the lion door guards, symbolising strength and dignity. On the right is usually a male lion pawing a ball, which is thought to represent the world. On the left, you often find a female with a cub under her paw. At the corners of most roofs are a parade of creatures often led by a man riding a hen. These were believed to discourage lightning from striking.

Shades of Meaning

Colours and multiples also have special significance. The yellow of the palace roof stands for the Earth; red walls represents fire, luck and happiness; blue and green mean spring and rebirth. Nine is a lucky number, reflected in the number of dragons on ramps and gold studs on doors.

Approaching from **Meridian Gate** (Wumen) are the three great halls and courtyards of the outer area. The **Hall of Supreme Harmony** (Taihedian) is the largest building in the palace, and also the first and most impressive of these. In its centre is the ornately carved golden Dragon Throne, from which the emperor ruled. Solemn ceremonies, such as the enthronement of a new emperor, were held here. The courtyard could hold 90,000 spectators. Behind the Hall of Supreme Harmony are the **Hall of Middle Harmony** (Zhonghedian) as well as the **Hall of Preserving Harmony** (Baohedian), complet-

ing a trinity reflecting the Three Buddhas and the Three Pure Ones of Taoism. To the east of the Hall of Preserving Harmony is the magnificent **Nine Dragon Screen** (Jiulongbi).

Facing the Nine Dragon Screen is the **Palace of Peace and Longevity**

Left: inside the Forbidden City. **Above:** detail of roofs and eaves
Right: the Palace of Heavenly Purity

(Ningshougong). Puyi lived in the palace until 1925, despite the founding of the republic in 1911. In 1932, he became the puppet emperor of Manchukuo, the Japanese name for their occupied territory in northeast China. Many palace treasures were stolen by the Japanese or taken to Taiwan by fleeing Nationalists, but the smaller halls to the east and west of the main halls still contain the impressive collections of the Forbidden City. A highlight is the clock and jewellery hall, with water clocks and richly decorated mechanical clocks.

Emperors and Eunuchs

On the other side of the imposing Outer Court, to the north and separated from it by the **Gate of Heavenly Purity** (Qianqingmen), lies a labyrinth of gates, doors, pavilions, gardens and palaces. This is called the **Palace of Heavenly Purity** (Qianqinggong), the residence of the imperial family, who were almost all exclusively female; the emperor and eunuchs were the only men permitted to enter.

After dropping off your cassette player near the **Gate of Divine Warrior** (Shenwumen), the north gate of the Imperial Palace, leave by Jingshanqian Jie, a street lined with food vendors. Try a Xinjiang-style mutton kebab and take a rest, before crossing to **Jingshan Park** (Coal Hill Park; open daily 7am–7pm; entrance fee). This is the best place to appreciate the sheer scale of the palace complex. The artificial hill was built with the earth dug from the palace moats in the early 15th century. In Qing Emperor Qianlong's day, the park was stocked with deer, hares, rabbits and thousands of songbirds. The last Ming emperor, Chongzhen, fled the besieged Forbidden City and hanged himself from a tree on Jingshan in 1644. A new tree has been planted on the same spot to record the event for posterity.

Above: view across the city from Jingshan Park

2. FRAGRANT HILLS PARK AND THE SUMMER PALACE
(see maps, below and p31)

Visit the peaceful Fragrant Hills Park and the Summer Palace in north-west Beijing, where emperors and poets retreated from the summer heat. Stop by the Sackler Gallery on your return. The tour takes a full nine hours.

The Fragrant Hills lie 28km (18 miles) northwest of the city. Allow one hour for a taxi ride from central Beijing.

From the 12th century to the 18th century, **Fragrant Hills Park** (Xiang-shan Gongyuan; open daily 8am–5pm; in summer 8am–sunset; entrance fee) was a favourite hunting retreat for the emperors, many of whom made their mark by building pagodas and temples here. At the height of its popularity, under the Qing emperor Qianlong, the walled park was full of exotic deer. Mao Zedong lived here briefly in 1949, at Shuangqing Villa, before moving to Zhongnanhai in Beijing's west. Much of the park fell into decay or was destroyed by European troops between 1860 and 1900, but it has since been restored and is now one of the most popular destinations for day-trippers from Beijing, particularly in the autumn.

Temple Walk

This walk involves some hilly, but not difficult, terrain, so wear strong shoes and get an early start. And if the weather permits, this would be a good opportunity for a picnic lunch. The ticket office is just left of the main entrance. Once inside, follow the stone path that veers right and buy another ticket to visit the Buddhist **Temple of the Azure Clouds** (Biyunsi; open daily 8am–4pm; entrance fee).

A temple was first built here in 1330 and later generations added new buildings, especially during the Qing dynasty. The first hall contains two huge celestial guardians, and the second a statue of the Maitreya Buddha, all from the Ming dynasty. The innermost hall is the **Sun Yat-sen Memorial Hall**, in memory of the leader of the Nationalist movement that overthrew the Qing dynasty. To the right of his statue is a crystal coffin, a rather macabre gift from the Soviet Union.

One of the temple's more unusual treasures is the Indian-style 35m (115ft) **Diamond Throne**

Fragrant Hills

400 m / 440 yds

- - - - Itinerary 2

Jingangbaozuota (Diamond Throne Pagoda)
Biyunsi (Temple of the Azure Clouds)
Sun Yat-sen Memorial Hall
Hall of 500 Luohan
Cable Car Ticket Office
Beimen (North Gate)
XIANGSHAN GONGYUAN (FRAGRANT HILLS PARK)
Jingxinhai (Chamber of Introspection)
Yanjinghu (Spectacles Lake)
Cable Car
Yuhua (Fourth Jade Flower Villa)
Liulita (Glazed Tile Pagoda)
Xishan Qingxue (Western Hills Shimmering in Snow)
Yuhua (Third Jade Flower Villa)
Zhaomiao (Temple of Clarity)
Xiangshan (Incense Burner Peak)
Pavilion of Varied Scenery
Dongmen (East Gate)
Chaoyang (Sun-Facing Cave)
Qiyue (Moonlight Villa)
Yuhua Shanzhuang (Jade Flower Villa)
Xiangshan Fandian (Fragrant Hills Hotel)
Lofty Phoenix Pavilion
Hongguang (Temple of Red Glow)
Banshanting (Pavilion halfway up the hill)
Jingcuiliu (Jingcui Lake)
Senyuhu (Tree-covered Imperial Audience Tablet, Jade Sceptre Cliff)
Yuxiang (Jade Fragrance Hall)
Hillside Pavilion
White Pine Pavilion
Red-Leaf Grove
Xiangshansi (Fragrant Hills Temple)
Shuangqing Shanzhuang (Twin Pools Villa)
N
Beijing

Pagoda at the rear of the complex. On the first level is a sanctuary with carved monster heads. This held Sun Yat-sen's body from 1925 to 1929, before it was moved to Nanjing. Climb up the inner stairs to the top terrace, with its central tower surrounded by six small pagodas covered in delicately carved *bodhisattva* (enlightened beings).

After descending and passing the Sun Yat-sen Memorial Hall, on your right you'll find the impressive **Hall of 500 Luohan**. Enter through the side gate in the lower terrace of this courtyard. The gilded wood statues (508 in all) represent legendary senior monks *(luohan)* who had achieved a higher insight into Buddhist truth and moral duty. Some of the statues meditate peacefully, one has a lion springing from his chest, while that of an old monk tears off his skin to reveal the face of a young man.

Park Peak

Walk down the hill from Biyunsi the way you came but turn right into Fragrant Hills Park proper just before you reach the exit. Another name for Fragrant Hills is **Incense Burner Peak**, a description of its appearance when fog settles on the 557m (1,827ft) summit. About 50m (55yds) along the path on the right is the ticket office for the chairlift (open daily 8.30am–5pm), substituting a 15-minute ride for an hour's steep climb. On the right you'll see the Diamond Throne Pagoda again, to the left is **Spectacles Lake** (Yanjinghu), named for its resemblance to a pair of spectacles, and beyond is the white glow of the luxurious Fragrant Hills Hotel.

After admiring the view from the pavilion on the summit, you have two choices. You can take the chair lift back to the bottom and head southward, visiting Spectacles Lake and the **Temple of Clarity** (Zhaomiao). Pass the east gate (but do not exit), walk several hundred metres along a leafy path that exits onto the main road leading to the Fragrant Hills Hotel. Turn right and walk 150m (165yds) to the hotel's main entrance.

If you have more energy, the path down from Incense Burner Peak starts at the end of the pavilion furthest from the chair lift terminus. The pleasant, and not particularly demanding path, zigzags its way through lush forest. On the way down – the walk takes about 40 minutes – stay right whenever the path forks. Halfway down you'll pass an old hunting lodge, two more pavilions and the ruins of the **Fragrant Hills Temple** (Xiangshansi), in the clutches of some gnarled pines.

Just beyond the temple, the path joins a road. Turn left and walk 100m (110yds) to the main gate of the **Fragrant Hills Hotel** (Xiangshan Fandian; tel: 10-6259 1166). This oasis of luxury, designed by Chinese-American architect I M Pei, embraces classical Chinese themes such as terraces, gates within gates and courtyards surrounded by halls, with modern angles and skylights. In the expansive grounds, an elaborately crafted Chinese garden blends into

Left: gilded statues, Pavilion of 500 Luohan
Top right: the Summer Palace

the wooded surroundings. The architecture is inspiring but the hotel itself is rather shabby and run-down.

On Mamaijie by the Fragrant Hills Hotel is a cafe-restaurant called **Sculpting in Time** (Sun–Thu 10am–10.30pm, Fri–Sat 10am–midnight), a pleasant spot for a coffee and a quick meal before heading in a taxi to the Summer Palace, about 10km (6 miles) away.

The Summer Palace

The **Summer Palace** (Yiheyuan; open daily, summer 6.30am–6pm, winter 8.30am–5pm; entrance fee) was built in the late Qing dynasty to replace the nearby old Summer Palace (Yuanmingyuan), which was destroyed by European allies in 1860 during the Second Opium War. The notoriously erratic Empress Dowager Cixi fulfilled a wonderful but expensive dream in 1888 when she created this sprawling playground – using 30 million taels of silver that was originally intended for the building of a naval fleet.

The debate continues as to Cixi's direct role in imperial China's decline, but the most widely accepted version of events begins as she was a concubine of the third rank. She placed herself on the Dragon Throne after the death of the emperor Xianfeng in 1861, and ruled unscrupulously for the next 50 years in the name of her child. In 1900, a large part of the palace was destroyed by the Europeans when the Boxer rebels laid siege to foreigners in Beijing.

As in every classical Chinese garden, water and mountains (usually rep-

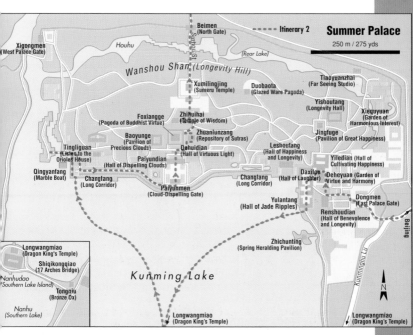

Summer Palace
250 m / 275 yds

resented by rocks) determine the landscape of the Summer Palace. The grounds cover more than 30sq km (10sq miles), three-quarters of which is occupied by **Kunming Lake**; but the following route takes in the highlights without wearing out your shoes. Inside the main gate, the lavishly furnished **Hall of Benevolence and Longevity** (Renshoudian) was where Cixi held audiences with ministers and handled other state business in the summer months. Behind it, veer right to the **Garden of Virtue and Harmony** (Deheyuan), with a three-storey open-air theatre at the centre. Here, Cixi used to enjoy operatic performances by her 384-strong ensemble of eunuchs. Using a system of trap doors between the stages, the eunuchs' elaborate productions featured immortals falling from the sky and evil spirits rising from the depths. The refurbished **Hall of Laughter** (Daxilou) opposite the theatre is where Cixi and her court sat to view the performances. The halls on the periphery of the court house many royal objects.

Taking the Dragon Boat

Backtrack to the **Hall of Jade Ripples** (Yulantang), on the edge of the lake, where you can buy a ticket for a tour by the 'dragon boat'. From the boat you can see the **Bridge of Seventeen Arches** (Shiqikongqiao) and the **Dragon King's Temple** (Longwangmiao) on a small island. The boat lands at the **Longevity Hill** (Wanshou Shan), where 150m (164yds) along the shore stands the famous **Marble Boat** (Qingyanfang), a folly in which Cixi once took tea.

If you don't feel up to a steep climb over the Hill of Longevity, continue in the same direction around the back of the hill, following signposts to the

shopper's paradise of Suzhou Street. Or walk back to the boat launch area to start an amble down the **Long Corridor** (Changlang). It runs for 700m (765yds) parallel to the northern shore of the lake, linking the scattered palace buildings. The light wooden construction is decorated with countless scenes from ancient Chinese mythology.

Halfway along the Long Corridor you'll come to a *pailou*, a triumphal arch, where you begin your ascent to the imposing Buddhist temple complex on the top of the hill. The **Hall of Dispelling Clouds** (Paiyundian) is where the Empress Cixi celebrated her birthdays, and some of her presents are displayed there. Beyond is the **Hall of Virtuous Light** (Dehuidian) and, up the winding stone stairs, the massive octagonal **Temple of Buddhist Virtue** (Foxiangge).

Adjacent, on the west side, is one of the few buildings that survived the destruction of 1900 undamaged, the **Pavilion of Precious Clouds** (Baoyunge). Though it looks wooden, its beams, columns and roof struts are made of cast bronze. The final short climb takes you to the **Temple of the Sea of Wisdom** (Zhihuihai), at the top of Longevity Hill. Built in 1750, it is covered with countless ceramic Buddhas. Many of the lower Buddhas were either smashed or beheaded by Red Guards during the Cultural Revolution. There are good views of the lake from this spot.

Suzhou and Sackler

Just behind the Temple of Wisdom, follow the upper path on the right side and then descend among the square towers and stupas of the **Sumeru Temple** (Xumilingjing) on your left. At its base, you'll find 'Little Suzhou Water Town'. The street was created as a replica of a 19th-century canal-side shopping area in Suzhou, to allow Cixi and her court to enjoy the pleasures of shopping without having to mix with ordinary mortals. It was restored in 1990 and is a kitsch end to your Summer Palace experience. Leave the Summer Palace on the north side of Suzhou Street.

If you have time on the way back to the city, visit the **Sackler Gallery** (open daily 9am–4.30pm; entrance fee) on Beijing University's beautiful campus. Enter by the west gate of the university. The gallery is the second building on the left after the bridge. View artefacts spanning 280,000 years, which for seven decades were stacked in the university's archaeology department. The display is well designed and the museum not too large, so you can pass from Paleolithic humanoids to the Qing dynasty in a matter of 45 minutes.

Top left: bridge over the western part of Kunming Lake
Left: Cixi's Marble Boat. **Above:** the Long Corridor

3. TEMPLE OF HEAVEN AND THE NATURAL HISTORY MUSEUM *(see map, below)*

Early morning exercise rituals in the Temple of Heaven park, followed by an exploration of the temple complex, a stop at the Natural History Museum and shopping at Hongqiao Market. This is a half-day tour.

Take a taxi to the north gate of the Temple of Heaven Park.

Enclosed by a wall 5km (3 miles) long, the **Temple of Heaven** (Tiantan; park open daily 6am–8pm; temple 8am–5pm; park entrance fee includes temple) is the best place in Beijing to catch a glimpse of some traditional, and some not so traditional, forms of Chinese culture. Along the paths or among the trees, *qigong* practitioners strengthen their internal systems through concentration and slow-motion exercises that stimulate breathing and circulation. Plan to arrive by 7am if you want to see early-morning enthusiasts of *qigong*, *taiji*, calligraphy, Peking opera and kite-flying. The temple complex was originally constructed between 1406 and 1429 under Emperor Yongle of the Ming dynasty. It was used for imperial sacrifices just twice a year: at the winter solstice, when the emperor thanked the gods for the last harvest; and then again on the 15th day of the first month of the lunar year (Lantern Festival), when he asked the gods to bless the coming harvest.

The Hall of Prayer for Good Harvests

The park is round in the north, representing Heaven, and square in the south, representing Earth. Find your way through it to the city's most elegant and most recognised structure, the **Hall of Prayer for Good Harvests** (Qinian-

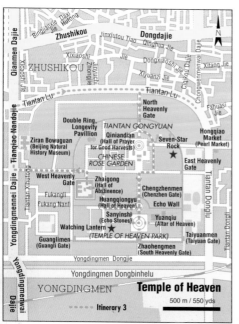

Temple of Heaven

500 m / 550 yds

···· Itinerary 3

dian), an exquisite example of a Chinese wooden building. Constructed without nails or cement, the round hall is 40m (130ft) high, its three levels covered with deep blue tiles symbolising Heaven. The roof is supported by 28 pillars: the four central pillars represent the four seasons; the double ring of 12 pillars represents the 12 months and the traditional divisions of the Chinese day, each comprising two hours, respectively. Intricate carpentry creates the dome high overhead; below are thrones where tablets commemorating the ancestors were placed. Destroyed several times, the hall was rebuilt in 1890.

Head south to the **Imperial**

Above: roof detail, Temple of Heaven
Right: the Imperial Vault of Heaven

Vault of Heaven (Huangqiongyu), much smaller but with similar deep blue roof tiles representing Heaven. The ancestral tablets were stored here until needed for the prayer ceremony. It is now best known for its acoustics. Stand on the first of the three **Echo Stones** (Sanyinshi), in front of the entrance, and clap; you will hear a single echo. Do the same on the second stone and you'll hear a double echo; and on the third, a triple echo. Whisper into the **Echo Wall**, enclosing the courtyard around the hall, and the other person will be able to hear every word anywhere along the wall. Walk south to the **Altar of Heaven** (Yuanqiu) where three concentric terraces stand inside two enclosures – one square (Earth) and one round (Heaven). Animal sacrifices took place inside the square enclosure while the emperor prayed at the centre of the mound.

Palaces, Museums and Markets

On the way to the west exit of the temple, you'll pass through the courtyard of the **Hall of Abstinence** (Zhaigong). The hall has a double moat spanned by a series of fine stone bridges, and its courtyard has a beautiful drum and bell tower. Twice a year, the emperor would spend a night of fasting and celibacy in the palace prior to the sacrificial rites the next morning. These rituals, which survived until 1914, go back 4,000 years. Leave by the west gate, just north of the Palace of Abstinence. Outside the gate, you'll run into the main north–south street, Tianqiao Nandajie, after walking about 100m (110yds). Turn right and walk about 300m (330yds) to the **Natural History Museum** (Ziran Bowuguan; open daily 8.30am–5pm; entrance fee), filled with many interesting and some bizarre exhibits.

A five-minute taxi ride will take you to the northeast corner of the park where, across the street, is **Hongqiao Market** (Hongqiao Shichang; open daily 8.30am–7pm). Built in 1995 to replace the old market that used to hug the park's wall, the new indoor market has everything, from meat, fish and spices to toys, clothes and antiques. For lunch, backtrack 400m (436yds) to the north gate of the Temple of Heaven. Across Tiantan Road you'll see **Yushan Restaurant** (87 Tiantan Lu; open daily 10am–2pm, 4.30pm–8pm; tel: 10-6701 4263) which specialises in Manchu-Han imperial banquets. Try the sesame cake with minced pork filling – this is the Chinese version of the hamburger.

4. Marco Polo Bridge, Ox Street Mosque and Fayuansi Temple *(see map, p18–19)*

The highlights of southwest Beijing, beginning with the Marco Polo Bridge in the suburbs of Wanping, and then a visit to two working religious centres. This is a half-day tour.

Take a taxi to Wanping, 15km (9 miles) southwest of Beijing.

In the 13th century, the Venetian merchant Marco Polo was on his way back to the West as an emissary of Kublai Khan when he encountered **Lugouqiao**, a 266-metre-long (873-ft) stone bridge spanning the Yongding River near the small town of Wanping. He gave it such rave reviews that Europeans dubbed it the **Marco Polo Bridge**. The bridge was built in 1189 during the Jin dynasty and rebuilt in the same style in 1698 after being badly damaged by a flood. Every one of its 140 stone columns is topped with an ornately carved lion; each of these stone lions is of a different size, and the smallest is just a few centimetres high. Emperor Qianlong added to the bridge's fame when he wrote the poem *Morning Moon over Lugou Bridge* in 1751.

The 'Marco Polo Bridge' Incident

You can see the emperor's poetry, in his own calligraphy, engraved on the steles next to the Marco Polo Bridge. This bridge was one of the main routes into the capital for camel trains and was used by motor traffic until the 1980s.

In Marco Polo's day, **Wanping** was a busy little riverside town full of inns and restaurants used by merchants. Under a grand scheme announced several years ago by the government, the old town was to be recreated, with facilities like a horse track, paddle boats and Qing-style homes. The city wall and gate towers were completed, but unfortunately the money then ran out.

The bridge is famous for the July 1937 'Marco Polo

Above and left: Marco Polo Bridge

Bridge Incident'. Japanese troops, who had seized control of a railway junction near Wanping, were fired on by Chinese soldiers. The Japanese, who already occupied northeast China and Taiwan, used the incident as a pretext for a full-scale invasion of Beijing and most of China. In the centre of Wanping, about 10 minutes' walk into town along the main street, is the **Memorial Hall of the War of Resistance Against Japan** (Zhongguo Renmin Kangri Zhanzheng Jinian Guan Bowuguan; open daily 8am–4pm; entrance fee). It contains an interesting pictorial history of the war from the Chinese perspective.

Get your driver to drop you at **Ox Street Mosque** (Niujie Qingzhensi; open daily 8.30am–5pm; entrance fee). Built in AD996, it has all the features of mosques elsewhere in the world – minaret, prayer hall facing Mecca and Arabic inscriptions – but in Chinese-style buildings. Islam reached China during the Tang dynasty (AD618–907) via Arab merchants, and Muslims now live in all parts of the country. This mosque is the oldest and largest of about 50 in Beijing.

Prayer takes place five times a day in the main prayer hall. There is a separate women's hall. Geometric designs and Arabic script adorn the walls inside, as the Koran allows no graven images, animal or human. The mosque is an active place of worship and a gathering place for Beijing's Muslim community, numbering about 250,000. Female visitors need not cover their heads to enter, but shorts or short skirts are not allowed (though the caretaker can lend you a pair of baggy pants) and non-Muslims cannot enter the prayer hall.

Temple of Buddhist Doctrine

The **Temple of the Source of Buddhist Doctrine** (Fayuansi; open 8.30–11.30am, 1.30–3.30pm, closed Wed; entrance fee), is a 15- to 20-minute walk from the mosque. Turn right on Ox Street (Niu Jie) as you leave the mosque. About 100m/110yds along, turn right again into Shuru Hutong. Walk along the street for about 500m/yds. Midway, you'll cross a wide street; here Shuru Hutong becomes Fayunsi Houjie. Turn right onto Xizhuan Hutong. Walk about 400m/yds and take a right into Fayuansi Qianhutong. The temple gate is 50m/yds along.

The Temple of the Source of Buddhist Doctrine is one of the oldest surviving and most pleasant Buddhist temples in Beijing. Built in AD645 it was formerly called Temple of the Loyal (Minzhongsi), to honour soldiers killed in battle. Today, it houses the Buddhist Academy, formed in 1956, devoted to training Buddhist novices who are then sent to monasteries across China. The academy has a library of more than 100,000 precious texts and an exhibition of Buddhist sculpture, some dating from the Han dynasty. Inside some of the temple halls are fine bronzes, some Ming dynasty, and a 6-m (20-ft) sleeping Buddha.

Right: roof detail at Niujie Mosque

5. WANGFUJING AND THE FOREIGN LEGATION QUARTER *(see map, p39)*

A morning tour of Beijing's premier shopping district, Wangfujing Dajie, followed by an architectural tour of early 20th-century Beijing through the former Foreign Legation Quarter. This route can either be done on foot (approx. 2½ hours), or by bike.

Take a car or the subway to Wangfujing.

Opposite the Beijing Hotel at the southern end of **Wangfujing Dajie**, the vast **Oriental Plaza** shopping complex is a mandatory shopping experience and is home to one of Beijing's finest hotels, the **Grand Hyatt Beijing**. Peruse the complex at your leisure and then stroll north up Wangfujing Dajie, past the huge Wangfujing Bookshop, perhaps diving left into the Wangfujing Xiaochijie (marked by a decorative archway), a busy quarter teeming with small restaurants and stalls serving dishes from all over China. Continue your walk if you wish up Wangfujing Dajie. The name Wangfujing dates back to the Yuan dynasty (1279–1368) when it was called Wang Fu Street; it later changed its name in the Ming dynasty, when a well *(jing)* was discovered. By the late Qing dynasty the street was a major commercial thoroughfare and many of Beijing's old brand names can be found here.

European Legacy

Early 20th-century European architecture in China is an instant reminder of the ignominious decline of the Qing dynasty and the foreign domination that followed. The **Foreign Legation Quarter**, south of Oriental Plaza and east of Tiananmen Square, contains many elegant European buildings that recall part of modern China's history. Between the 1860s and the outbreak of the Sino–Japanese War in 1937, 13 foreign governments were represented here, their presence forced on the Chinese by the outcome of the Opium Wars. They had their own administration, police, churches, hospitals, shops and post office, guarded by some 1,000 soldiers. After 1900, when the Boxers launched

Above: the coffee shop in the Beijing Hotel

a 45-day attack here, the area was closed off to Chinese nationals.

To get there, backtrack south to Oriental Plaza, cross over Dongchang'an Jie and head down Taijichang Dajie (Customs Street). About 200m/yds along on the right, at No. 1 you'll come to the gate of the former **Italian Legation**, where the Italians relocated in 1900 after the Boxer rebels destroyed their previous quarters. It now houses the **Chinese People's Association for Friendship with Foreign Countries** (CPAFFC).

House of Many Owners

Continue along Taijichang Dajie but cross to the opposite side. Walk alongside a high gray wall topped with curved tiles and turn left into the first alleyway. About 200m/220yds on the left is the gate to the former **Hungarian Legation**, now the **Institute of International Studies**. Built in 1900, the simple grey and white building has changed hands many times. In 1915, when China declared war on Germany and its allies, the building was occupied by the Hungarians. After a short spell under the Dutch, a Russian general turned it into a guesthouse in the late 1920s. In 1938, it became the German Club. The Americans used it for Allied Property Administration and it later became the Hungarian Embassy. The building was finally returned to the Chinese in 1969.

Double back to Taijichang Dajie and turn left. Through the first gate on the left is an elegant grey-blue building with arches along the ground floor, topped by a red national emblem and a single portal. This is the headquarters of the **Beijing People's Congress** (no entry to the public). Built in 1902, it was once the **Peking Club**, with a swimming pool and tennis courts that were still in use as late as the 1960s. The white building opposite, topped with an enormous red star, is the headquarters for the Beijing municipality Communist Party Committee.

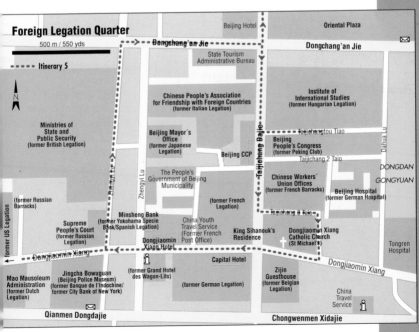

Foreign Legation Quarter

500 m / 550 yds

- - - - - **Itinerary 5**

N

Beijing Hotel

Oriental Plaza

Dongchang'an Jie

Dongchang'an Jie

State Tourism Administrative Bureau

Chinese People's Association for Friendship with Foreign Countries (former Italian Legation)

Institute of International Studies (former Hungarian Legation)

Ministries of State and Public Security (former British Legation)

Beijing Mayor's Office (former Japanese Legation)

Beijing CCP

Taijichangtou Tiao

Beijing People's Congress (former Peking Club)

Taijichang 2 Taio

DONGDAN

GONGYUAN

Zhengyi Lu

The People's Government of Beijing Municipality

(former French Legation)

Chinese Workers' Union Offices (former French Barracks)

Beijing Hospital (former German Hospital)

Taijichang 6 Taio

(former Russian Barracks)

Supreme People's Court (former Russian Legation)

Minsheng Bank (former Yokohama Specie Bank/Spanish Legation)

China Youth Travel Service (Former French Post Office)

King Sihanouk's Residence

Dongjiaomin Xiang Catholic Church (St Michael's)

Dongjiaomin Xiang

Tongren Hospital

former US Legation

Dongjiaomin Xiang

Dongjiaomin Xiang Hotel

Capital Hotel

Zijin Guesthouse (former Belgian Legation)

China Travel Service

Mao Mausoleum Administration (former Dutch Legation)

Jingcha Bowuguan (Beijing Police Museum) (former Banque de l'Indochine/ former City Bank of New York)

(former Grand Hotel des Wagon-Lits)

(former German Legation)

Qianmen Dongdajie

Chongwenmen Xidajie

Moving along Taijichang Dajie, you'll enter 'Little France'. The French, along with the British, were the first to install permanent diplomatic representatives here. They held large tracts of land on both sides of the street. On the right side of the street are the graceful roof lines of the former **French Legation**. Turn left at the second alleyway, about 200m/yds beyond the Peking Club. French theologian Teilhard de Chardin, who lived in China from 1932 to 1946, founded an institute of geobiology on this street. Much of this area has been replaced with typical Chinese apartment blocks, but about 100m/yds along on the left, you can peer through the gates of the former **French Barracks**. The Soviet-style building at the centre is now the **Chinese Workers' Union** offices.

Continue another 100m/yds along this alleyway and turn right. After another 100m/yds, you will reach **Dongjiaomin Xiang** (Legation Street). Turn right again. Just before the next junction, about 200m/yds along on the right, is **St Michael's Church**, an intimate little neo-Gothic church built by the French Vincentian Order in 1902. St Michael's was closed after the 1949 revolution, but was renovated and reopened in 1989. Services are held daily, and the staff and congregants are happy to let you stroll through to visit or pray. The figures of the saints above the chapel doors date all the way back to 1889 and some of the stained glass and ceramic tiles are original too.

More Overseas Legations

Opposite the church, you can see the jagged brick roof lines and green tops of the former **Belgian Legation** (now the Zijin Guesthouse). Before 1900, this was the home of a high level Chinese official, Xu Tong, who hated foreigners so much that he purportedly wished to cover his sedan chair with their skin. He did his best to avoid the barbarians, but when the Allied armies entered Beijing in 1900 in reaction to the Boxer Rebellion, Xu Tong could take it no longer. He committed suicide.

From St Michael's, cross Taijichang Dajie and continue along Dongjiaomin

Xiang. Approximately 50m/yds past the junction, where two massive stone lions and two armed soldiers stand guard, are the red gates of another building belonging to the former **French Legation**. This is the former occasional residence of Cambodian King Norodom Sihanouk, a favour from the Chinese government when he went into exile. Next door is the home of Premier Wen Jiabao.

Across the road is the gate to the former offices of Jardine Matheson, one of the earliest and most aggressive Western trading companies in Asia.

About 200m/yds further along Dongjiaomin Xiang, you'll pass a tiny building on the right with fancy brickwork, a zigzag roof line and arched windows.

Left: St Michael's Church

This is now a Sichuanese restaurant, but was originally the French Post Office and was also the site of the original Beijing Hotel before it moved to its current location in 1900.

Next to it is the beginning of the former **Spanish Legation**, where the protocol on the Boxer Rebellion was signed in 1901. The Spanish sold the corner lot to the Yokohama Specie Bank. Currently, the building houses the **Minsheng Bank**. Empress Dowager Cixi was said to have borrowed money here just before the last dynasty fell. The valuables she put up as collateral were never reclaimed and are now in a collection in London. The bank stands on the corner of Dongjiaomin Xiang and Zhengyi Lu, the divided north–south street. Zhengyi means 'justice', but the road used to be called Canal Street because there was a trench that carried sewage water. It was filled in 1925 to create the promenade between the two lanes.

Cross Zhengyi Lu and continue on Dongjiaomin Xiang. On the right is the site of the Russian Orthodox Mission, and was later the **Russian Legation** and then the Soviet Legation. Until 1991, there was a simple stone building here, probably the former Russian church. The newly expanded **Supreme Court** now stands here. Opposite it is the **Police Museum** (Jingcha Bowuguan; open Tues–Sun 9am–4pm; entrance fee) with exhibits and a 'laser shooting' game. About 300m/yds further down on the left side of the street, you will find a brick structure with a green roof. The building, formerly the **Dutch Legation**, is now the office of the **Mao Mausoleum Administration**.

The British Legation

Retrace your steps along Dongjiaomin Xiang and turn left on Zhengyi Lu for the final stretch. The area on the right side of Zhengyi Lu, north of the Minsheng Bank, was the **Japanese Legation**. It now houses the **Beijing Mayor's Office** and the offices of the city government.

The last, and possibly grandest relic on this walk is further along Zhengyi Lu on the left: the former **British Legation**. The British moved in after the Second Opium War of 1860 and expanded the area to create the largest territory held by foreigners. They retained this compound until 1959, but it is now occupied by the **Ministries of State and Public Security** – the Chinese version of the KGB – the Ministries picked up some of the original buildings, moving them further west to make room for new offices.

The Legation loop brings you to the corner of Zhengyi Lu and Dongchang'an Jie, across from the Beijing Hotel.

Above: Huacheng Finance Corporation
Right: former Japanese Legation

6. LAMA TEMPLE, CONFUCIUS TEMPLE AND DITAN PARK
(see map, p18–19)

An introduction to two different Chinese philosophical traditions, followed by dinner and dancing at Ditan Park. The three sites are all within a 1-km (½-mile) radius so the tour is an easy walk or bicycle ride.

Take the subway to Yonghegong station. After leaving the station via the south-east exit, turn left onto Yonghegong Dajie. The main gate of the Lama Temple (Yonghegong) is 100m/yds along on the left.

Buddhism came to China from India as early as the 1st century, but Lamaism, the mystical sect of Tibetan Buddhism that incorporates shamanist beliefs and practices, only gained influence in the eastern part of China after the Mongols conquered Tibet and China in the 13th century. The Manchus practised Lamaism, so its influence revived under the Qing dynasty.

The Lama Temple

Originally the private residence of Prince Yong, the **Lama Temple** (Yonghegong; open daily 9am–4pm; entrance fee) was turned into a monastery after its owner became Emperor Yongzheng in 1723. According to ancient Chinese custom, the former residence of a Son of Heaven had to be dedicated to religious purposes once he left. Therefore, in 1744, Yongzheng's son, Emperor Qianlong, established it as a Lamaist monastery, and it soon flourished as a centre of Lamaist religion and art. At the same time, the monastery offered the Qing rulers welcome opportunities for influencing and controlling Tibetan and Mongolian subjects. It remained a monastery until 1960.

The temple, the most elaborately restored sacred building in Beijing, belongs to the Yellow Hat sect, whose spiritual leader is the Dalai Lama. Since the Chinese invasion of Tibet in 1950, relations between the authorities and Buddhist leaders have been problematic. The current Dalai Lama fled to India in 1959 after failing to win independence for Tibet. He is still condemned by Beijing, but his image, once forbidden, can now be displayed in temples. The government officially remains atheist, but during the reforms

since 1978, temples and churches have been restored, along with the right to worship.

The Lama Temple has five halls and three gates laid out along a north–south axis. In each successive hall, the central Buddha is more imposing than the last; in the three-storied section of the fifth hall, **Pavilion of Ten Thousand Happinesses** (Wanfuge) is a 23-m (75-ft) statue of the Buddha carved from a single piece of sandalwood. Today, about 70 monks live here.

Lamaism's roots lie in the mysterious rituals of the ancient Tibetan Bön religion. Look closely at the carvings and Tibetan *thangka* paintings in the side halls. One image shows the goddess Lamo riding a horse cloaked in the skin of her own son, sacrificed to show her detachment from the world.

The Temple of Confucius

Next stop is a tranquil former centre of scholarship, the **Confucius Temple** (Kong Miao; open daily 8.30am–5pm; entrance fee). Go west on Guozijian Jie, the street opposite the Lama Temple across Yonghegong Dajie. The entrance to the Confucius Temple is 200m (220yds) on the right.

In its glorious past, emperors came to offer sacrifices to Confucius at the Hall of Great Achievement, hoping for guidance in ruling. Confucius was a teacher in the state of Lu (in present day Shandong province) in the 6th century BC, about the same time as Buddha was teaching in India. The brand of Confucianism adopted by the emperors stressed order, and so, Confucianism was an important tool for keeping order across the vast and diverse nation.

Built in 1306 during the Yuan dynasty, this is the second-largest Confucian temple in China, after the one in Confucius' hometown, Qufu. The temple's prize possession is a collection of 190 steles (upright stone tablets) inscribed with records of ancient civil service examinations.

Leave the temple, turn right and walk 200m/yds along Guozijian Jie for a brief look at the former **Imperial Academy** (Guozijian; open daily 8.30am–5pm; entrance fee), now the Capital Library. Once the highest educational institution in the land, thousands of students and scholars came here to listen to the emperor expound Confucian classics. A set of steles commissioned by Emperor Qianlong records 13 Confucian classics. The 800,000 characters were engraved by a single scholar over 12 years.

Should you require a beverage, EJE (open daily 2pm–midnight), a cafe located in a former courtyard home is at 20 Guoxue Hutong, just east of the north gate of the Confucius Temple.

By this time, you'll be ready for earthly pleasures: food, song and dance. Proceed to **Ditan Park** (Ditan Gongyuan; open daily 6am–9pm; entrance fee) by returning to Yonghegong Jie and walk-

Left: Lama Temple, Gate of Honour **Above:** Confucius Temple pavilion
Right: Confucius Temple stone stele

ing north under the Second Ring Road. The south entrance to the park is 300m/yds north of the Yonghegong subway station, to the left. **Jing Ding Xuan** (daily 24 hours), next to the entrance, serves tasty dim sum. **Ditan** (the Altar of the Earth; daily 8am–5pm; entrance fee), first built in 1530, had a similar ritual function as the Temple of Heaven. Each year, on the summer solstice throughout the Ming and Qing dynasties, the emperor came here to make sacrifices. The altar, a round platform surrounded by two concentric square walls where the sacrifice was offered, was restored in the 1980s.

Feng Ze Xuan (daily 11am–2pm, 5–8.30pm; tel: 6429 2666), west of the altar, serves Southern Imperial food to a predominantly tour-group clientele. Reserve – and order – in advance. Though Jin Ding Xuan is a safer

(and more affordable) bet, it doesn't offer transport through the park in golf-cart-buses. After dinner, join one of the popular pastimes of modern China, ballroom dancing. 'Dance parties' are held daily (6.30–11am, 7–10pm from May–Oct; 6.30–11am Nov–May; entrance fee) at **Lie Yuan Flower Garden**, 200m (220yds) north of the altar. The park officially closes at 9pm but the gate is open all night to accommodate ballroom dancers. The park also holds one of Beijing's best Spring Festival temple fairs, with performances including Peking opera, folk dancing, re-enactments of Qing dynasty imperial rituals, as well as stalls selling traditional snacks. For more contemporary revelry just outside the park's south gate, **Tango** (daily 24 hours) has a disco, chill-out lounges, a huge live venue and karaoke, all under one massive roof.

7. DAZHALAN AND LIULICHANG *(see map, p18–19)*

A walk through fascinating *hutong* (alleyways) south of the Foreign Legation Quarter and Tiananmen Square. The route will take between one and three hours depending on whether you stop to shop.

This walk continues from the vicinity of the Wangfujing Dajie and Foreign Legation Quarter Walk described on pages 38–41. Alternatively, you could take the subway to Chongwenmen then walk 500m/yds west along Chongwenmen Xidajie.

Walk southwards along Ximi Hutong (which runs south from Chongwenmen Xidajie) for around 100m/yds before turning right onto Xidamochang Jie. Then you must head west for about 250m/yds to the **Beijing Underground City** (open daily 8am–5.30pm; entrance fee), which is on your left at 62 Xidamochang Jie. This is the access point to an enormous subterranean network of bomb-proof tunnels and shelters which was built between the 1960s and 1970s on the instruction of Chairman Mao at the height of the Sino–Russian rift.

Above: Peking opera at Lie Yuan Flower Garden

Guides are available for tours through the clammy tunnels and you can make out the signs leading the way underground to the Forbidden City and other landmarks. Although only a section of the tunnel is open for exploring, it is enough to give you a good idea of the scale of this vast undertaking.

Continue heading west along Xidamochang Jie for almost 1 km (½-mile), cross Qianmen Dajie and then turn left onto **Zhubaoshi Jie** (Jewellery Street) running parallel to Qianmen Dajie . But before you dive into the *hutong*, make a note of Quanjude's flagship outlet (daily 11am–1.30pm, 4.30–8pm), just south of the archway over Qianmen Dajie, the disneyland of Peking Duck restaurants.

There are bargains galore here, although some of the products are of poor quality. With hawkers shouting prices from all sides, music blaring, and egg vendors and pedicab drivers pushing their way through the crowd, it's easy to imagine Dazhalan at the turn of the 20th century.

Prostitution in Dazhalan, once a deeply entrenched feature, has all but disappeared under communism. There were various classes of brothels, and during the Nationalist period the women were registered and given regular health checks. The economic reforms of the 1980s and 1990s have seen prostitution make a gradual, if less visible, comeback in Beijing (although not in Dazhalan) and other Chinese cities. The authorities generally ignore it so long as it is restricted to the usual venues – hairdressing salons, massage parlours and hotels.

Clothing and Fabrics

About 300m/yds or so further along, Zhubaoshi Jie intersects with **Dazhalan Jie**, a wide and bustling alley with a green police booth on the left side of the corner. Turn right, then 20m/yds along on the right you will see a building with extravagant wrought-iron gatework in green: **Yi Chen Hou** (open daily 9am–8.30pm). Check out the wide choice of fabrics on the second floor.

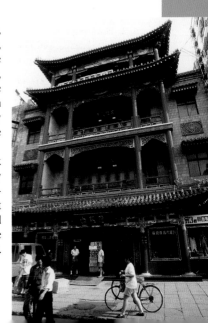

The same goes for the **Ruifuxiang Silk and Cotton Fabric Store** (open daily 9am–8pm) two doors down, with a pretentious marble entrance. Ruifuxiang was built here in 1893 by a Shandong businessman and catered to society's upper crust, including the wives and concubines of the Imperial Court.

Above: colourful Dazhalan bazaar
Right: a store on Dazhalan Xijie

beijing & environs

At No 22 Dazhalan Xijie is the **Zhang Yiyuan Tea Shop** (open daily 8am–8pm) with bas-relief flower designs under its windows. Next door at No 24 is the **Tongrentang Traditional Medicine Shop** (open daily 8am–7.30pm), once responsible for keeping secret medicinal recipes for the emperor. It's been here since 1669 and the pharmacist still weighs age-old herbal remedies with a hand-held scale. Look out for the incredible array of cures, from deer antlers and whole newts to ginseng for curing impotence and enhancing the libido.

A little further down, at No 34, is an ornate and traditional Chinese-style four-storey building, the **Neiliansheng Shoe Store** (open daily 8.30am–8pm), built in 1853. There is nothing traditional about the chrome and glass interior displays with the latest shoe styles. You can be shod cheaply, but only if your feet are fairly delicate, an American size 8 (UK size 6) or smaller in women's sizes.

Communal Living

Now walk about 300m/yds along Dazhalan and you will arrive at another junction with a little green police booth. Turn right and then, another 30m/yds

or so further on, turn left. This is **Yangmei Alley**, a typical Beijing *hutong* with children and old people in the street and the smells of cooking and communal toilets mingled together. Most of the doors lead into *siheyuan*, courtyards with rooms on four sides facing inwards. Life in these houses is not very comfortable. In summer, the heat drives the inhabitants out to the streets. In winter, most homes are heated by coal-burning stoves.

After another 400m/yds, Yangmei Alley takes a little jog to the right, where you will see an antiques shop on your left. Turn left to **Liulichang**, a restored section of the old city, which is undergoing yet another restoration, jam-packed with curios, carpets and antiques. This has been a shopping area for books and antiques for more than 300 years.

During the Ming dynasty, Liulichang, which means 'glazed-tile factory', was one of the sites where tiles were made for the imperial buildings. Later, it was developed into a cultural centre for scholar-officials who came here to stock up on calligraphy materials, books and seals. More recently, Liulichang was synonymous with music shops, from traditional to heavy metal. Most shops have since relocated, but **Tom Lee**, a Hong Kong-based superstore at 120 Zhushikou Xidajie (daily 9am–5.30pm), still is a top source.

Check out **Rongbaozhai** (open daily 9am–5.30pm), a 17th-century shop at No 19 Liulichang Xijie, which is famous for its range of watercolour block paintings, charcoal rubbings and reproductions of old paintings.

Above: gallery in Liulichang

8. THE LAKE DISTRICT *(see map, p18–19)*

Explore the area around the ancient Drum and Bell Towers, and walk along the lakes to the imperial gardens of Beihai Park. Walk, or cycle if you prefer. This half-day tour is designed for the afternoon, but can easily be adapted for the morning.

Take a taxi to the Drum and Bell Towers. You'll spot the towers just north of the junction of Di'anmen Dajie and Gulou Dongdajie.

Browse around the *hutongs* around and between the Drum Tower and the Bell Tower. You'll find lots of Beijing's signature snack foods: *haobing* (griddle-fried cakes with sesame seeds on top), *qiehe* (fried stuffed eggplant), *chao tianluo* (fried river snails), *jianbing* (crepes) and *douzhi* (milky dough made from beans). Stick to hot-off-the-stove food if you don't wish to risk an upset stomach.

The Bell and Drum Towers

The grey **Bell Tower** (Zhonglou) and the red **Drum Tower** (Gulou) (both open daily 9am–4.30pm; entrance fee) are the legacy of Kublai Khan. He had the original ones built nearby to serve as the imperial clock. The Drum Tower used to hold 24 giant drums. They were beaten to mark the closing of the city gates and the passing of the night watches. The bell struck the time of day. As with most Mongol buildings, the towers were replaced in 1420 during the Ming dynasty. The Bell Tower, which was made of wood, burned down and was rebuilt of stone in 1747.

The 33m (108ft) Bell Tower is more interesting structurally. Its stone staircase leads through a dark passageway reminiscent of medieval castles. In 1990, the bell was re-installed in the tower. Since then the mayor has climbed the tower at every Spring Festival to ring in the Lunar New Year. A chief attraction of the Drum Tower is the view from the top over the surrounding area of traditional

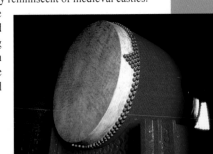

Above: view from the Drum Tower
Right: one of the drums at the Drum Tower

beijing & environs

siheyuan courtyard houses. In the hall at the top is one original drum, damaged during the Opium Wars, flanked by two replicas.

To start your walk around the lakes, go south on Di'anmen Dajie and turn right on the first alleyway you come to, about 50m/yds along. This is

Yandai Xiejie, which has become a major part of the Houhai scene, packed as it is with tiny café-bars and knick-knack shops *(see Nightlife, page 71)*. Another 150m/yds along is a junction where you should make a left turn. Ahead is a stone bridge that divides **Houhai** (Rear Lake) from **Qianhai** (Front Lake). The two are part of a string of six lakes extending all the way from the north to the south of the old Inner City.

Lakeside Stroll

Cross the little stone bridge and turn left on the road that runs along the shore of Qianhai. The lake draws swimmers in summer (and some in winter), skaters in the winter and strollers all year round. Here you will encounter pedicabs offering *hutong* tours, a comfortable way of checking out the alleyways around the lake. Expect to pay 180 yuan for 2½ hours. But getting lost in the alleys on foot is a great way to see the neighbourhood; alternatively, there are many bike rental outlets around the lake. **Lotus Lane**, located at the southwest corner of Qianhai past several bar strips, features not only a Starbucks, but also some shopping and high-end bars. **South Silk Road** (daily noon–11.30pm) has great Yunnan food, while, across the lake, **Han Cang** (daily 11am–2pm, 5–10pm) has fantastic Hakka cuisine. The square beside Starbucks hosts nightly dancing and a variety of daytime activities – music, massages and more.

Cross Di'anmen Xidajie to the north entrance to **Beihai Gongyuan** (North Lake Park; open daily 6.30am–8pm; entrance fee). The area around the lake served as imperial residence for every dynasty that had its capital in Beijing. After the end of the imperial era in 1925, Beihai Park was opened to the public, though **Zhongnanhai** (Central and Southern Lake), surrounded by a thick wall, remain the cloistered domain of the Chinese leadership.

Zhongnanhai is today the site of the Politburo and State Council offices. Also known as the 'New Forbidden City', it is closed to the public.

The park is a relaxing place for strolling in and going out on the lake in a rented rowboat. The focal point, however, is **Jade Island** (Qiong Dao), once the site of the winter residence of Kublai Khan – but first skirt the western shore to see the **Nine Dragon Screen** (Jiulongbi), one of three in the city, and said to offer protection from fire.

Next stop, about 200m/yds along the shore, is **Miniature Western Heaven** (Xiaoxitian), built in 1770. Aptly named, it was a shrine to Guanyin, the goddess of mercy. It's a large square pagoda surrounded by a moat and four guard towers. Backtrack to the **Five Dragon Pavilion** (Wulongting), named after the zigzagging walkways that link them.

Ferry to Jade Island

Just north of the Five Dragon Pavilion board a ferry to **Jade Island** (Qiong Dao; every half hour, 9am–6pm). The boat stops in front of Fangshan Restaurant, a potential dinner (or lunch) destination – but first explore the imperial gardens.

The restaurant is in the **Hall of Ripples** complex. Turn right on the covered walkway that leads to the **Pavilion of Shared Coolness**, and take the stone path leading up the hill. Climb to the **Plate for Gathering Dew**, there's a bronze figure of a man holding a container over his head. Emperor Qianlong built this whimsical tribute to a Han dynasty emperor who believed the dew was an elixir for immortality. Along the northwest side of the hill is the **Building for Reading Old Inscriptions** (Yuegulou), which has stone tablets covered with 6th- and 7th-century calligraphy. At the island's summit is the dazzling **White Dagoba** (Baita), a 35-m (115-ft) Buddhist shrine dating from 1651, built by the first Qing emperor to commemorate the first visit to Beijing by a Dalai Lama.

Descend the south side of the hill and pass through the **Hall of Universal Peace** (Pu'andian), an official meeting room in the Qing dynasty. Last is the Lamaist **Temple of Eternal Peace** (Yong'ansi). When you emerge at the south side of the island, you'll be facing an elegant marble bridge connecting the island to the shore. From here you can see, or cross the bridge to visit, the **Round Town** (Tuancheng; open daily 8.30am– 4.30pm; entrance fee). It used to be the administrative centre of the Mongol Yuan dynasty in 15th-century Dadu.

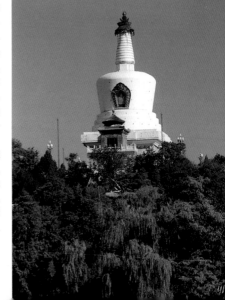

The imperial cuisine at **Fangshan Restaurant** (open daily 11am–1.30pm, 5–8pm; tel: 10-6401 1879) features sculpted beancurd with vegetables, bird's nest soup and more. Leave Beihai Park by the south gate, where taxis wait.

Top left: market snacks. **Left:** Nine Dragon Screen. **Right: the** White Dagoba

9. PEKING DUCK AND PEKING OPERA *(see map, p18–19)*

A classic night on the town. Indulge in the ritual of eating Peking roast duck and then proceed to watch Peking opera.

Get to Tiananmen Square. Zhengyangmen Quanjude Roast Duck Restaurant is on the east side, just opposite the Monument to the Heroes of the People. Call ahead for reservations if you are with a large group (44 Dongjiao Minxiang; tel: 10-6512 2265; open daily 11am–2pm, 5–8pm).

The earliest mention of Peking duck can be traced back to a 12th-century cookbook. The chefs from **Zhengyangmen Quanjude Roast Duck Restaurant** are schooled by Beijing's Quanjude masters, whose predecessors opened the famous Qianmen Quanjude Restaurant a few blocks to the south in 1864.

To prepare the ambrosial Peking duck, the bird's unbroken skin is inflated like a balloon, filled with water and glazed with sugar. The duck is then roasted in an oven heated by burning the wood of fruit trees such as date, peach and pear. This is done in order to impart a sweet, earthy aroma to the skin and flesh. When cooked, the crisp skin is sliced into bite-size pieces and served with a thin pancake, spring onion and a salty *hoisin* bean sauce. The rest of the duck meat is used in other dishes accompanying the meal. Part of the art of this cuisine is to make use of the entire duck, and this restaurant claims to make more than 300 different duck dishes, to be sampled while the duck is being roasted. If you're adventurous, try the cold mustard duck web, deep-fried duck liver with sesame and the fried duck hearts with chili sauce, but give the duck soup (à la dishwater) a miss.

When the roast duck arrives, you fill your own pancakes at the table. Use your chopsticks to pick up some spring onion and use it as a kind of paintbrush to dab some sauce on the pancake. Add one or two pieces of duck, roll the pancake, and *voila*! This is one of the rare times in China when using your fingers to eat is not considered impolite, so enjoy it. The cost of

Above: the art of make-up is all-important in Peking opera

a meal at the restaurant is approximately 80 yuan per person, including a few different duck dishes and a drink.

A sort of 'Best of' Peking opera can be found at the Qianmen Hotel's **Liyuan Theatre** (175 Yong'an Lu; performances daily 7.30–8.45pm; tel: 10-6301 6688, ext 8860), a 10-minute taxi ride from Qianmen. You can buy tickets from the booth next to the car park.

Peking opera is so highly stylised that you might assume it's an ancient art form, but in fact it was created in the late 18th century, drawing from several regional theatre forms. The result is a feast for the senses, though some find it an acquired taste. The singers use high-pitched voices and notes are strung out, the face-paint and costumes outrageous, and the action on stage accompanied by a piercing string and percussion ensemble.

Opera Conventions

In general, Peking opera can be classified into two types of stories – civilian and military. The Qianmen Hotel stages Peking opera mainly for foreign visitors, so they tend to choose action-packed martial stories, as well as excerpts from the classic novel *Journey to the West*, a popular Buddhist epic about the travels of the monk Tripitaka to seek Buddhist scriptures in India. These are great fun because the characters wear colourful costumes and there are plenty of acrobatics to dramatise battles. If you still have difficulty following the story, the English subtitles will help.

The characters with painted faces called *Jing* are warriors, heroes, statesmen, adventurers and supernatural beings. Good guys are generally painted with simpler designs, while more complicated patterns indicate enemy generals, bandits and robbers. Colours will tell if a character is courageous (red), cruel and conniving (oily white), wise (purple), or other-worldly (gold). Some painted designs tell a story, like the suns painted on the face of Hou Yi, the legendary character who shot down nine suns. Aside from the *Jing*, there are three main character types: *Dan*, a female lead role traditionally played by a man; *Sheng*, the male lead role; and *Chou*, the clown.

Much can be surmised from the body language of the performers, costumes, movements and props – all of which have set meanings. A single candle might represent evening, while a soldier carrying a banner represents an entire regiment. The flick of a sleeve expresses disgust. Like other traditional arts in China, Peking opera is losing ground to popular TV, film and music, but there is still a small, dedicated audience, mostly of older people, who relish it.

Other places to enjoy Peking opera, which are perhaps not as touristy as Liyuan Theatre, include **Changan Grand Theatre** (7 Jianguomennei Dajie; tel: 10-6510 1310 ext 10) and **Huguang Huiguan** (3 Hufang Lu; tel: 10-6351 8284). Call in advance to check on the performance times.

Right: Peking duck

10. TIANANMEN EVENING *(see map, p18–19)*

A sunset walk beginning with the flag-lowering ceremony on Tiananmen Square; then a walk by the moat of the Imperial Palace, ending with a visit to a night market, shopping in Wangfujing and out on the town.

Tiananmen's flag-lowering ceremony happens at sunset, around 7.30pm in summer and 5.30pm in mid-winter. This is one of the few remaining Soviet-style rituals China still practises. To encourage patriotism after the Tiananmen crackdown in 1989, the ceremony was beefed up with more soldiers and a new taller flagpole. Hundreds gather each night to watch the military drill and flag-lowering; thousands on May 1 and October 1, although it's hard to know precisely what draws them. A favourite pastime in Beijing is to *kan renao*, which basically means to 'watch the excitement'. This could be anything from a lovers' tiff to a minor traffic accident. At any rate, soon after the flag descends, quiet settles over the square. At night, after the lights come up on the Monument to the People's Heroes and Tiananmen Gate, the square seems a very different place.

Gateway to the Forbidden City

Begin your walk by crossing under Dongchang'an Jie via the pedestrian tunnel, and then walking through **Tiananmen Gate**. The long approach from the gate, leading to the Meridian Gate (Wumen), the entrance to the Imperial Palace, is about 600m (655yds), at which point you will be forced to turn. Turn right and walk along the perimeter of the Imperial Palace, between its high wall and the moat. Strolling with just a few bicycles whirring past and lovers whispering on park benches, it is easy to imagine you have been transported back to a different century.

Go right, leave via the side gate and take an immediate left. This road runs between the palace and

Above: Tiananmen Gate by night
Right: red bean porridge for supper

the moat, so you cannot get lost. After 50m/yds, it turns right, goes straight for another 400m (437yds) and turns left where there is another 50-m/yd stretch. At this point you will see the east gate of the Imperial Palace on the left. Here you'll also find **The Courtyard** gallery and restaurant (gallery: daily 11am–midnight; restaurant: daily 6pm–midnight, Sunday brunch noon–2pm). The gallery showcases avant-garde art, while the latter is one of the top-rated restaurants in the city. On the third floor, the cigar lounge is a great place for a pre-night-market drink. The road bends right and becomes **Donghuamen Night Market**. Here, you will find some of the most varied snacks in town. Try a bowl of red bean porridge or grilled quail if you're feeling peckish. Adventurous souls have no end of options for critters on sticks.

If you still need a full meal, you're in luck as you've just reached a strip of restaurants largely owned by and catering for overseas Chinese. There is good seafood and Cantonese fare on both sides of the street. Splurge on braised shark's fin with creamy crab sauce at the swanky **Hong Kong Food City** (on the right side; you can't miss the neon; 18 Dong'anmen Dajie; open daily 11am–midnight; tel: 10-6525 7349). Or try Mongolian hotpot at any one of the small restaurants along this stretch – you get plates of thinly-sliced raw meat and vegetables to plunge into a pot of boiling stock. Much of the pleasure derives from eating food you've just cooked yourself.

Shopping and Nightlife

After dinner, continue walking east to Wangfujing, Beijing's foremost shopping street *(also see pages 38–41)*. Head north up Wangfujing Dajie to **St Joseph's Church**. Also known as the East Cathedral and illuminated at night, it was originally built in the 17th century, has been restored many times and recently spruced up into a main feature of the district. To round off the evening, hop into a taxi and check out the nightlife, scattered among densely-packed bar neighbourhoods. **Sanlitun** is the perennial choice: 'Bar Street' is a strip of bars that run along Sanlitun Lu, north from Gongti Beilu, just east of the City Hotel. Here you'll find almost a dozen identical scenes: Chinese businessmen out on the town, playing dice games and listening to trios cover pop classics from China and abroad. Further east, at **Chaoyang Park's** east gate, is a bar neighbourhood comprising

mainly foreign businesspeople. Behind Women's Street's strip-mall of restaurants, in the midst of the new embassy district, lies **'Super Bar Street'**. The north gate of the Workers' Stadium hosts Mix and Vic's, while a visit to **Wudaokou**, with its bargain booze and international student bodies, is just the ticket to relive your college days *(see also Nightlife, page 77)*.

Right: street stalls, Donghuamen Night Market

Excursions

1. MING TOMBS AND THE GREAT WALL AT MUTIANYU
(see maps, p56 and 58)

A morning exploring the Ming tombs, followed by a picnic at the ruins. Then, a spectacular drive through the mountains and an afternoon hike on the Great Wall at Mutianyu. This is a full eight-hour day with strenuous walking.

Ask your hotel staff to help you rent a taxi for the day. This is a 185-km (115-mile) round trip and should cost approximately 300 yuan. Make sure the cost, duration and itinerary are agreed in advance. And make sure your driver understands that you want to go to the Great Wall at Mutianyu, not the teeming Badaling section. A clearly marked road leads directly from the Ming Tombs to Mutianyu.

Of the 16 Ming emperors who reigned from 1368 to 1644, 13 were buried about 50km (30 miles) northwest of Beijing, in a natural amphitheatre formed by mountains on three sides. Heading due north from the Deshengmen Gate, you will retrace the route followed by the imperial dead to their final resting place. About 40km (25 miles) outside the city, you will pass through **Changping**, once a garrison town partly responsible for guarding the tombs. The town has a monument to the peasant leader Li Zicheng, who led the uprising that toppled the Ming dynasty in 1644.

Spirits of the Dead
When you reach the Ming Tombs (Shisanling; open daily 8am–6pm; entrance fee), enter through the **Spirit Way** (Shendao), the path over which the dead were carried during the funeral ceremony. It begins with a white stone portico a few kilometres north of Changping and stretches nearly 6km (4 miles) to the gate of the central tomb. The entrance to the imperial graveyard, which covers 15½ sq km (6 sq miles), is 500m (550yds) beyond the portico at the **Great Palace Gate** (Dagongmen).

Just beyond it is the entrance to the **Avenue of Stone Figures**. Ask the driver to let you walk and pick you up at the other end. Experts still debate the symbolism of these 24 carved stone creatures. Two of these, the *xiezhi* and *qilin*, are two varieties of the Chinese unicorn – mythical animals that may have been placed there for luck. The more familiar elephants, camels and horses were probably meant to serve the emperors in the afterlife. Beyond the animals are 12 stone people: four fierce soldiers, four officials and four scholars.

Left: the Great Wall at Mutianyu
Right: Avenue of Stone Figures, Ming Tombs

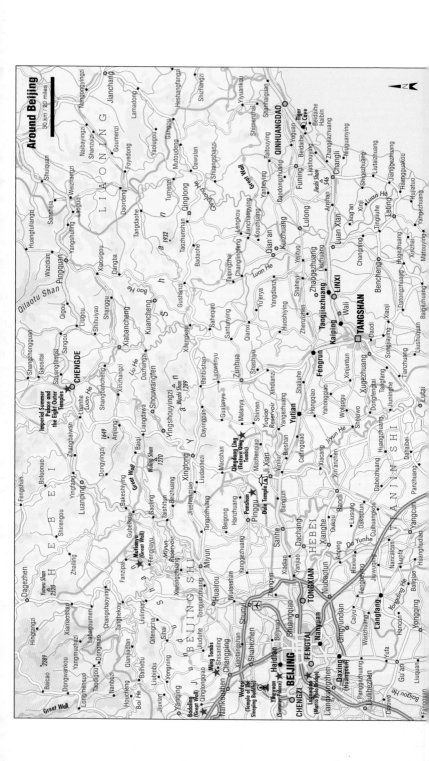

Three of the 13 tombs in this area are officially open as tourist sites: Dingling, Changling and Zhaoling. This excursion takes you to the first two, plus the ruins of another, Deling. Make your first stop about 10 minutes from the Avenue of the Animals at **Dingling** (open daily 8am–6pm), burial site of Emperor Wanli (1573–1619). His is the only tomb in this area that has been excavated. Wanli spent 8 million silver taels on his bid for immortality, enough to feed a million people for 6½ years at the time. It took 30,000 labourers six years to build the subterranean palace of five rooms with graceful arched ceilings – which were full of gold, silver, porcelain and jade treasures at one time.

Tombs with a View

To reach the vaults, cross the courtyard, climb the **Square Tower** (Fang Cheng) and follow the paths behind. The first room you enter has a pedestal that was intended for Wanli's concubines, but it was mysteriously empty when opened. According to one theory, this room was left empty for fear that repeated opening of the tomb would allow evil winds to disturb the emperor.

The next large room contains three stone altars, which were pushed up against the huge stone slab doors leading to the room where the coffins of Wanli and his two wives lay along with 26 treasure chests. Some of the

treasures are displayed at Changling, your next stop. More lasting is the architectural genius invested in the graves by the Ming emperors. The massive stone doors, now behind glass, were designed so that another stone slab slid into place when closed, locking them from the inside.

Move on to **Changling** (open daily 8am–6pm), a five-minute drive to the northwest. The burial place

Above: pavilion of the Great Stele
Left: Changling

of Emperor Yongle (1403–24), this is the best preserved of all the 13 tombs and a good example of how they were organised. In the front section, a large courtyard dominated by twisted pines leads to a sacrificial hall. The **Hall of Eminent Favours** (Ling'endian) is supported by 32 giant pillars, each carved from a single tree. The yellow glazed tiles and dragon head drains symbolise imperial majesty. A funeral tablet used to lay on a wooden altar at the centre of this room and sacrifices were made in front of it. The hall now contains an exhibition of items found in Dingling, from jewelled hairpins to suits of armour and the rich dragon brocade used in imperial dress.

Buried Pleasures

The second section is a courtyard in which a large stele marks the grave of the emperor. Just behind is the burial mound, enclosed by a wall about 500m (550yds) long. Presumably, this contains Emperor Yongle's coffin and burial treasures. To the east and west are burial grounds for his 16 concubines who, by some accounts, were buried alive to bring pleasure to the emperor in the next world.

Last stop at the tombs is Deling, where you part company with the vendors; you may want to buy drinks before leaving Changling. **Deling**, a 10-minute drive southwest, is where Wanli's grandson, Emperor Xi Zong (1621–27) is buried. Known as a keen carpenter but an inattentive ruler, Xi Zong lost power

Above: unrenovated Ming Tombs

to his eunuchs. His dilapidated, overgrown tomb seems to reflect his downfall, with ceremonial urns strewn around as if after a brawl.

Backtrack to Changling. In the far corner of the car park, 100m (110yds) from the entrance, is a sign in Chinese saying 'Great Wall at Mutianyu 37km'. This is a beautiful drive eastward through villages and mountains. It is slightly further than the crowded Badaling section, but worth the effort.

You will spot the **Great Wall** long before you reach it. Adding together all the sections, it extends more than 3,860km (2,400 miles), twisting and doubling back from the coast all the way to the northwestern province of Gansu. Chinese tourist leaflets assert that this is the only man-made structure visible from the moon, but it is rumoured that New York's Staten Island garbage dump now shares the honour. Whatever the case, the Great Wall is a terrific lookout point for a soldier, or a tourist. The walk up to the wall takes a good 20 minutes, but you can avoid the climb by taking the cable car.

The 'Ten Thousand Li Great Wall', or *Wanli Chang Cheng* in Chinese, marked the peak of wall building in China. The wall originated as a labyrinth of smaller walls built by warring kingdoms in northern China from the 5th century BC. The first Qin emperor, Shi Huangdi, after unifying China in 221BC, made it his mission to link all the existing walls to create a single Great Wall against the barbarian tribes to the north.

Wall of Bones

Like the pyramids, the wall has its dark side. Hundreds of thousands of Chinese peasants were conscripted to build it, and many died in the process. Poets lamented the wall's 'bone core'. As many raids and later the full-scale Mongol invasion proved, a wall is only as strong as those who defend it. Nevertheless, once the Ming overthrew the Mongol Yuan dynasty, wall-building resumed with a vengeance. This was when the Great Wall took shape. **Mutianyu** and most other remaining sections date from the Ming period (1368–1644), when the wall was extensively repaired and fortified, with several new sections added. The restored Mutianyu section opened to tourists in 1986.

The section formerly known as the 'Wild Wall', **Huanghuacheng**, will not be wild for much longer as renovation plans are underway. A four-hour moderate to heavy hike takes you through spectacular scenery from Simatai to Jinshanling. Simatai also has a cable car for the less hiking-inclined. There are also many other 'unofficial' wall sites that locals can point you toward; while the wilder sections are officially off-limits, it's tough to keep watch on the entire structure.

The road back to Beijing heads 75km (46 miles) due south, entering the city at Dongzhimen.

Right: the Great Wall at Mutianyu

2. BEIDAIHE BEACH AND SHANHAIGUAN *(see map, p56)*

A relaxing getaway to the seashore at Beidaihe on the Bohai Sea. This is an overnight trip because of the long train ride, especially if you want to also see the Great Wall meeting the sea at Shanhaiguan.

Ten trains run daily from the Beijing Railway Station to Beidaihe and Shanhaiguan. The fastest take three hours from Beijing to Beidaihe and a little longer to Shanhaiguan. Trains that go via Tianjin take around five hours. Book tickets a few days in advance. If making this a winter trip, skip Beidaihe and head straight to Shanhaiguan.

If you've conquered Beijing's temples, or they've conquered you, and you've had enough of the capital's crowds and traffic, then it's time for a day on the beach. Located at the southwest of Qinhuangdao Municipality, Beidaihe is a famous summer resort, which charms with its seaside views, small-town ambience and bustling night stalls. The route there is a well-worn

path for Beijing's officials and politicians, escaping the capital's summer smog. Top leaders are usually cloistered away at a private beach south of town. The main beaches are packed in July and August, but remarkably clean. On the hills overlooking the Bohai Sea are mostly old brick villas with verandahs. A small boardwalk area is home to some good, inexpensive seafood restaurants. The best hotel deal for foreigners is the **Beidaihe Guesthouse for Diplomatic Missions** (1 Baosan Lu; tel: 0335-404 1287; open Apr–Oct), a five-minute walk from the main beach. It has friendly, English-speaking staff and a good seafood restaurant. All rooms have sea-facing balconies. The **Jiaohai Hotel** (97 Dongjing Lu; tel: 0335-404 1388) is a three-star option.

Shanhaiguan

Consider also spending the night in Shanhaiguan, a short bus or taxi train ride 25km (16 miles) north of Beidaihe along the coast. This walled, former garrison town marks the Great Wall's culmination at the sea. You can climb onto the ramparts at the First Pass Under Heaven in town, or make your way to a more interesting stretch of wall snaking up the hills at Jiaoshan not far north of Shanhaiguan; or join the wall as it reaches the sea at Old Dragon Head to the south. The **Jingshan Hotel** (Dong Dajie; tel: 0335-505 1130) is right by the First Pass Under Heaven; or try the **Shanhaiguan Grand Hotel** (107 Guangcheng Nanlu; tel: 0335-506 4488) just outside the town walls, not far from the station. You can take a direct train back to Beijing without having to return to Beidaihe.

Above: Beidaihe is one of China's most popular beach resorts

3. CHENGDE *(see maps, below and p56)*

An overnight stay in Chengde, the eclectic mountain retreat of the Qing emperors. With a four-hour train journey from Beijing, you might want to consider a second or even a third night at Chengde to cover its numerous and varied sights.

Chengde, 250km (115 miles) north of Beijing, is connected by 3 trains daily from both the Beijing Railway Station and the Beijing South Railway Station. The railway in Chengde is on the south side of town. Taxis and motorcycle taxis are both cheap and plentiful and can take you directly to your hotel.

Emperor Kangxi (1662–1722) of the Qing dynasty was drawn to the town of Jehol, as Chengde was called in the early 18th century, because of its location in a cool, lush valley with placid lakes and forests, 350m (1,148ft) above sea level. He ordered the building of the **Mountain Manor for Escaping the Summer Heat** (Bishushanzhuang) in 1703, which turned the previously obscure town into an imperial resort, with a regal garden that was the largest in China. Remnants of it can still be viewed today. The manor was also used in the later years of the Qing dynasty, when Emperor Qianlong (1736–96) expanded the residence, incorporating the styles of China's minorities in his sprawling kingdom as part of an effort to appease them.

Magical Retreat

In the Yanshan Mountains that surround the resort were 11 active temples, varying in architectural style. **Bishushanzhuang** (open daily 8am–6pm; entrance fee) is an excellent escape and a magical place to explore. If you have just one night in Chengde, spend the first afternoon strolling through Bishushangzhuang and save the more strenuous exploration of the temples for the next morning.

If you have more time, bizarre rock formations, caves and hot springs await you in the outlying areas. Chengde is quite compact and Bishushangzhuang can be reached easily by foot from the hotels. Public buses and minibuses

Above: the Tower of Mist and Rain, Bishushanzhuang

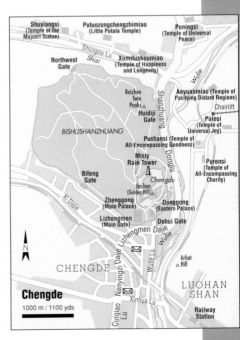

Nos 2, 3 and 5 also run up the main road, Wulie Jie, and stop next to the main gate of Bishushanzhuang.

Little in Chengde is translated for non-Chinese speakers. You may want to hire a guide through the local branch of the China International Travel Service (CITS; 11 Zhonghua Lu; tel: 0314-202 6418). The Yunshan Hotel can also arrange a guide.

Just inside the main gate is the **Bishushanzhuang Museum** (open daily 8am–5pm; entrance fee), which once housed the main palace. Laid out in the traditional linear style of halls and courtyards, it is made of unpainted wood and shaded by tall pines. The exhibits are varied: some rooms display items like Mongolian weapons and dress, others are set up as they were when they were used by the imperial court. Leaving by the back door of the museum takes you to the park proper. It is surrounded by a 10-km (6½-mile) wall and is the largest surviving imperial garden in China.

Pavilions and Pagodas

Off to the right, after 100m (110yds), begins a maze of paths, bridges, pavilions and halls surrounding several interlocking lakes. This area is for strolling, renting boats or gazing from park benches. Beyond it is the **Literary Nourishment Pavilion** (Wenjinge), one of four imperial libraries. Its central attraction is a rock garden where there is a special place for permanently 'viewing the moon', a trick of the light falling on the surrounding rock formations. At the far end of the east side of the park, you'll find a meadow marked by the pagoda of the **Temple of Eternal Blessing**, which was built by Emperor Qianlong for his mother's 50th birthday.

Heading left from the lake takes you into more rugged hiking area. Emperors Kangxi and Qianlong designated 72 scenic spots in Bishushanzhuang but you can find many more yourself. The hills are riddled with small temples and rock formations and topped by pavilion look-out points. A good place to relax and enjoy the greenery is the tea garden at the southeast corner of **Front Lake**, the main lake.

Get an early start on your second day and head for the temples (open daily 8am–5pm) beyond the walls of Bishushanzhuang. A good way to do this is to rent a taxi for the morning or day. Hiring a bike is also a good strategy as you can visit a selection of temples, and the scenery is excellent. A number of hotels rent bicycles, including the Yunshan Hotel.

The full circuit comprises the Eight Outer Temples, but start with these four and see how time and energy hold out. **Little Potala Temple** (Putuozongchengzhimiao; open daily 8am–5.30pm), which dates from 1767, is the largest and most spectacular complex, modelled on the Potala in Lhasa. The beautifully restored halls, staircases and walkways extend over a 22ha

Above: Tibetan architectural styles at Puningsi

excursions

(54 acre) hillside site. Tibetan-style prayer flags, banners and tapestries hang from the gleaming gold roofs of the temple. The design of the **Temple of Happiness and Longevity** (Xumisfushoumiao; open daily 8am–5.30pm), 1km (½ mile) east, is based on another Tibetan temple, at Shigatse. Built in 1779, it is still being restored. At its rear is one of the highlights, an octagonal pagoda commemorating the 70th birthday of Emperor Qianlong.

The **Temple of Universal Peace** (Puningsi; open daily 8am–5.30pm), 3km (2 miles) further northeast and built in 1755, stands out as it is a living monastery with about 50 lamas in residence. The second hall is laid out with long, low benches for religious study and ceremony. There is an amazing 22-m (72-ft) carved wooden statue of Guanyin, the Goddess of Mercy, with 42 arms and an eye on each palm (known as the Thousand Arm, Thousand Eye Guanyin). Finally, trek to the **Temple of Universal Joy** (Pulesi; open daily 8am–5.30pm), which lies due east of Bishushanzhuang. You'll find bronze images of the deities in various acts of passionate embrace and conquest of their enemies, great examples of the wonderful and terrifying imagery that comes with Tibetan Buddhism.

Club Peak Rock Formations

One of the strangest rock formations in the area is at **Club Peak**. You get there by taking a cable car from a few hundred metres north of Pulesi. It takes 20 minutes each way.

There are some good places to stay in Chengde, such as the three-star **Yunshan Hotel** (2 Bandisuan Lu; tel: 0314-205 5588), the popular **Mountain Villa Hotel** (11 Lizhengmen Dajie; tel: 0314-202 3501) near the Bishushanzhuang and the **Qiwanglou Hotel** (1 Bifengmen Donglu; tel: 0314-202 4385), a reproduction of a Qing-dynasty mansion. A different option, if you're visiting between March and October, is the **Mongolian Yurt Holiday Village** (tel: 0314-216 3094). Inside the imperial resort grounds, you stay in circular Mongolian tents (yurts). It's not real camping as the yurts are air-conditioned and have baths and television sets, but it's fun.

Local cuisine centres mainly on wild game, as the area was reserved as the emperor's hunting ground. Try **Huanggong Yushanfang** at the **Palace Hotel** (21 Wulie Lu; tel: 0314-207 5092). Women dressed as Qing dynasty maids serve venison, wild boar and pheasant. Ask for prices in advance; they're not listed on the menu. Staying in your hotel for meals is a safe, but less interesting, option; there are snack vendors and restaurants near the temples and Bishushanzhuang, but these would not win any awards for cleanliness.

Above: Club Peak
Left: Mongolian-style yurt

EATING OUT

ood is one of the most important parts of
fe in China, and borders on the obsessive,
kely a result of the not-so-distant past, when
etting enough to eat was a challenge. But
eijing has come a long way, and is repre-
entative of the high value and variety placed
pon the culinary arts. In 2003, there were
0,000 registered restaurants in the capital,
5,000 percent increase from 1976.

The range of eating options is enormous,
rom street vendors roasting sweet potatoes
or a few yuan to Western restaurants dish-
ng up meals that are significantly costlier.
'or the tourist, Beijing offers cuisines from
he country's various regions and from
round the world at reasonable prices.

The approximate cost of a meal per per-
on is categorised as follows:
$ = 50–100 yuan;
$$ = 100–200 yuan;
$$$ = more than 200 yuan.

Beijing and Imperial Cuisine

Many dishes classified as Beijing-style actu-
lly originated from other parts of the king-

dom, and were perfected and embellished
at the imperial court. Beijing cuisine makes
liberal use of strong flavours like garlic, gin-
ger, spring onion and coriander. The dishes
of the north tend to be heartier, with noodles and steamed or fried bread as the staple,
rather than rice.

Jianbing, Beijing's most popular street
snack, originated in Tianjin. It is a kind of
pancake made with egg and spring onion,
filled with crunchy, deep-fried dough sticks
and garnished with chili sauce and coriander. The most famous Beijing dish is Peking
duck, a whole meal with many dishes featuring every part of the duck it is possible
to eat *(see page 50)*. Another popular meal,
especially in winter, is Mongolian hotpot –
slivers of mutton plunged into a trough of
boiling water, fondue-style.

Li Family Restaurant
*11 Yangfang Hutong, Deshengmennei Dajie,
Xicheng*
Tel: 10-6618 0107
Serves four tables of up to 12 each day –
two at lunch and two at dinner in the home
of the chef, who has a story for each dish.
Book ahead. Open daily 4.30–10pm. $$$

Fangshan Restaurant
Qiong Dao, Beihai Park, Xicheng
Tel: 10-6401 1879
Garden setting at Beihai Park *(see page 49)*.
Opened in 1925, this restaurant is best at
creating an authentic Qing atmosphere.
Note: Qing court cuisine does not always
appeal to modern taste buds. Open daily
11.30am–1.30pm; 5–8pm. $$

Mei Fu
*24 Daxiangfeng Hutong, south bank of
Houhai.*
Tel: 10 6612 6847
Beijingers are notoriously anti-Shanghai,
but they relish the southern city's food. This
courtyard-cum-Shanghai salon is one of the
nicer places to be a hypocrite. Open daily
11.30am–2pm, 5.30–10pm. $$

Xiao Wang's Home Restaurant
2 Guanghua Dongli; 4 Gongti Beilu
Tel: 10-6594 3602; 6592 5555
Cheerful, centrally located restaurant, offer-

Above: Beijing-style dishes

ing home-style dishes (and Peking Duck) that appeal to foreign clientele in a comfortable, relaxed ambience. Open daily 11am–2pm; 5–11pm. *$–$$*

Old Beijing Noodle King
29 Chongwenmenwai Dajie, Chongwen
Tel: 10-6705 6705
Close to the Temple of Heaven, this restaurant has revived the lively tradition of Beijing fast food. Waiters bellow at the diners to announce the arrival or departure of each customer. Try the tasty noodles, usually eaten with a thick sesame and soy-based sauce. Look for the rickshaws outside. *$*

Peking Duck Restaurants
Tuanjiehu Peking Roast Duck Restaurant
3 Tuanjiehu Beikou, Dongsanhuan
Tel: 10-6582 2892
At one of the classiest of duck restaurants, every part of the duck is served in a range of exquisite side dishes including deep-fried heart with coriander and stir-fried intestines. The roast duck is a little crisper than that of many competitors. *$$$*

King Roast Duck
Opposite Friendship Store, Jianguomen Dajie
Convenient for a post-Ancient Observatory-at-dusk-dinner. Try the minced duck lettuce wraps and other duck-related appetisers – in addition, of course, to the main event. *$$*

Sichuan Cuisine
The densely populated southwester province of Sichuan is famous for its spic food, which, it is said, matches the temper ament of its people. Sichuan restaurants ar found everywhere in Beijing, and Sichua dishes are standard on most menus in smal non-specialised restaurants. Chicken, por and freshwater fish are favourite ingredients and noodles, bread and rice are all served. Tr some *dandan mian* (hot spicy noodles) or *l mian* (cold spicy noodles), peppery *shuizh yu*, or the sizzling rice-crust dish, *guo ba*.

Sichuan Restaurant
14A, Liuyin Jie, Xicheng
Tel: 10-6615 6925/6924
Formerly located in a *hutong* behind th Great Hall of People and frequented by th former Chinese Premier Deng Xiaoping, thi well-known restaurant can now be found nea Prince Gong's Palace, north of Beihai lake The food is still as delicious. Try the Sichua spicy and sour soup, and diced chicken wit hot peppers. Reservations should be made Open daily 11am–2pm; 5–9pm. *$$*

South Beauty
11 locations across town including: Pacifi Century Place; China World; Orienta Plaza; Kerry Centre
Tel: 10-6539 3502; 6505 0809; 8518 6971 8529 9458

Above: clear soups are typically Chinese

Upscale restaurant popular with the business crowd both for lunch breaks and dinners to impress. Open daily 11am–11pm. $–$$

Fei Teng Yu Xiang
Various locations including: 36 Xingfu Yicun Xiang (north end of parking lot opposite Workers' Stadium); 1/F Yehuaye Building near south gate of Scitech
Tel: 10-6415 3764; 6515 9600
Chain restaurant featuring *shuizhu yu*, chunks of fish in a huge bowl of peppers and chilli sauce. Open Mon–Fri 11am–10pm, Sat–Sun 11am–10.30pm. $

Cantonese Cuisine
Cantonese food is known for its delicate flavours and fresh ingredients, preferably bought the same day and cooked briskly before serving, using little oil or spice. *Dim sum* – rice-flour or bread parcels filled with meat, seafood or vegetables – are meant to be snacks but come in so many varieties that a *dim sum* lunch often turns into a feast. Many excellent Cantonese restaurants have sprung up in Beijing, but they tend to be more expensive than other Chinese restaurants.

East Ocean Seafood
89 Maizidian Jie, Chaoyang (near Lufthansa Centre)
Tel: 10-6508 3482
The Cantonese clientele should be your first clue to this restaurant's authenticity and prowess. The seafood is fresh, and the *dim sum* a great bet. Open 11am–11pm. $

Otto's Restaurant
14 Di'anmen Xidajie (opposite Qianhai); Chaoyang Park west gate
Tel: 10-6405 8205; 6593 1078
Budget-priced, high-quality Cantonese fare featuring the non-dim-sum end of the spectrum: noodles, soups, and *bifentang* – meats, seafood and veggies covered in deep-fried garlic chips – dishes. Open 24 hours. $

Other Chinese Cuisines
Red Capital Club
66 Dongsi Jiutiao
Tel: 10-6402 7150
Dine in elegance at this renovated courtyard home, as the Red-Guard-uniformed

wait staff patiently waits for diners to read the short story accompanying each of the items on the thick menu. Grab a pre- or post-dinner cocktail in the cigar lounge seated in the furniture of former leaders. Reserve ahead. Open daily 6–11pm. $$$

Afanti
2 Houguaibang Hutong, Chaoyangmennei Dajie, Dongcheng
Tel: 10-6525 1071
Lively Xinjiang restaurant serving sumptuous roast lamb, kebabs and flatbreads. Live music and dancing usually inspires patrons to jump atop their tables to join in the fun. Reservations advised. Open daily 11am–midnight. $$

Women's Street
Nuren Jie, Dongfang Qicai Shijie, opposite the Israeli embassy
Before you hit Super Bar Street, visit the range of restaurants including Xinjiang, Sichuan, Korean BBQ, Japanese, Malaysian, hot pot and more. Ignore the touts screaming at you from all ends, pick a spot and dig in. $–$$

Gongdelin
158 Qianmen Nan Dajie, Qianmen
Tel: 10-6511 2542
Beijing's most famous vegetarian restaurant. The Beijing branch of a Shanghai restaurant which opened in the early 1920s, Gongdelin specialises in amazing mock meat dishes, carefully crafted from beancurd, mushrooms and vegetables. A few dishes are so realistic that some vegetarians are put off by the appearance. Open daily 10.30am–1.30pm; 4.30–8pm. $

Han Cang
East bank of Qianhai, north of Ping'an Dadao
Tel: 10-6404 2259
Featuring the cuisine of the Hakka minority, and the place where Beijing's cool get their grub. Try the clay-pot eggplant and the foil-wrapped fish, both featuring some of the tastiest sauces in town. Open daily 11am–2pm, 5–10pm. $

Makye Ame
All Xiushui Nanjie, behind Friendship Store

Tel: 10-6506 9616
Authentic food, comfy couches and general cosy atmosphere, until the nightly song and dance show, which treads the line between cheese and fascination. Open 11.30–2am. *$*

Other Asian Cuisines

Hatsune
Heqiao Dasha, 8A Guanghua Lu (east of the Kerry Center)
Tel: 10-6581 3939
Hip, sleek Japanese joint with a soundtrack and inventive *sushi* menu to match. Three restaurants under one roof, featuring, respectively: *sushi*, BBQ and hotpot. Open 11.30am–2pm; 5.30–10pm. *$$*

The Taj Pavilion
China World Trade Centre
Tel: 10-6505 2288 ext 8116
Relaxing Indian restaurant with a large and convincing menu. It may be rather expensive, but both the ambience and the dishes are excellent. Open 11.30am–2.30pm; 6–10.30pm. *$$*

Lau Pa Sak
Northwest corner of intersection of Xindong Lu and Dongzhimenwai Dajie, opposite the Canadian embassy
Tel: 10-6417 0952
South Asian noodle, rice and curry dishes, with a smattering of dishes inspired by Singaporean street food. The sweet coffee is a must-try. Open daily 11am–11pm. *$*

Nam Nam
7 Sanlitun Lu

Tel: 10-6468 6053
Vietnamese food served in a comfortable and cool setting. *$*

Western

Alameda
Sanlitun Beijie (beside Nali shopping centre)
Tel: 10 6417 8084
Great *prix fixe* menus featuring multiple courses of fantastic Brazilian food and cocktails to match. Open 10.30am–11pm. *$$*

Courtyard
95 Donghuamen, Dongcheng
Tel: 10-6526 8882
A renovated courtyard-type house, with sleek modern interior, skylights and a cigar lounge. The chic restaurant overlooks the moat of the Imperial Palace. Serves well prepared East-West fusion cuisine in an atmosphere of casual elegance. Downstairs is a contemporary Chinese art gallery. This is an oasis if you need to be pampered. Reservations recommended. Open daily 6pm–midnight (last order at 9.30pm), Sunday brunch noon–2pm. *$$$*

Flo
2/F Rainbow Plaza, 16 Dongsanhuan Lu (East Third Ring Road, north of the Changhong Bridge)
Tel: 10-6595 5139
Beijing's original French restaurant, and one of the most authentic. Open 11am–3pm; 6–11pm. *$$*

Grandma's Kitchen
11A Xiushui Nanjie (behind Friendship Store); B/0103 Jianwai SOHO, 39 Dongsanhuan Zhonglu
Tel: 10-6503 2893; 5869 3055
Grandma's Kitchen is just as it sounds – American home-cooked meals and desserts are featured. Open 7.30am–10pm. *$*

Traktir
1A Xiyangguan Hutong, Beizhong Jie (one street north of Ghost Street/ Dongzhimennei Dajie)
Tel: 10-6403 4835/36 ext 118
Great Russian favourites are served here in a ski-chalet-esque atmosphere. Open 11.30am–11pm. *$*

Left: breakfast at a street stall

NIGHTLIFE

'Beijing nightlife' was once a contradiction in terms, but as China opens up and its people have more time and money for leisure, even the puritanical capital is beginning to shake a little. Some traditional forms of entertainment, like the teahouse and the night market, are reviving. New forms, especially pubs, discos and live music, have caught on among the younger and more affluent population.

If you want to do as Beijingers do, the first place to go is where the food is: night markets and restaurants. Night markets are fair weather spots where you can sit outside, eat snacks and swill cool beer. When the weather's colder, seek out Mongolian hotpot, which follows the Chinese proverb of 'making one thing serve two purposes' by warming your hands as you cook your own dinner.

Ballroom dancing made a strong comeback in the 1980s and remains popular among middle-aged and elderly people and occurs on street corners or at community and park gates. Karaoke remains second only to eating in popularity, even among the city's hip and trendy. Cinemas are plentiful but movies are a hit and miss affair. Famous Chinese art house films shown in the West, like *Farewell My Concubine* or *Raise the Red Lantern*, are not typical of the Chinese and Western action movies shown in most cinemas in Beijing. Beijing likes its neighbourhoods: Copycat bars vying for predominantly dice-playing, tea-drinking crowds grow like fungus in 'bar streets' across town. Hotels are far from the only source for discos and live music, though recent renovations have put hotel bars back on the radar. Bands and DJs of all stripes – both local and imported – play regularly around town and thanks to committed promoters and organizers, Beijing is becoming something of a regular stop on the international circuit.

Beijing remains a casual place. Formal dress is not required anywhere, though neatness is appreciated in expensive hotels and restaurants. For such a large city, Beijing is very safe, but take the usual precautions with valuables as the number of pickpockets appears to be increasing. Men alone or in groups should beware of 'clip joints', bars in which hostesses will join you for a drink and later demand huge fees for their 'services'.

Gay bars or nightclubs, as with most other Asian countries, tend to be low key and underground. There are a few uniquely gay watering holes, but the locations do change on occasion. It's best to surf the Internet for information before arriving in China to see what is on and where. Long-time spots include über-disco Nightman, east of the Exhibition Centre, on Xibahe Nanli; and Half Bar, at the north end of the street that runs along the east side of the Yaxiu market.

Above: a Beijing disco scene

Beijing's rapid pace of change is exemplified in its nightlife scene. The only way to keep up with what is going on is through local English-language entertainment guides, such as the excellent *that's Beijing*; other regular publications include *City Weekend* and *Time Out*. You can pick them up for free at various hotels, restaurants and bars. Or check the following web listings: www.thatsbeijing.com, www.cityweekend. com.cn, www.xianzai.com. Tickets for many cultural events in Beijing, including theatre, music, ballet and Peking opera, can be bought on-line from www.webtix.com.cn.

Night Markets
Donghuamen Market
One block west of Palace Hotel
Offers good range of Beijing snacks, critters-on-sticks, Cantonese sweets and more. Closes about 10pm.

Ghost Street
Dongzhimennei Dajie, from the Second Ring Road to Beixinqiao
Not technically a market, but a strip of restaurants slowly returning to its former glory that draws the dinner and late-night hordes.

Ballroom Dancing
Qianhai
Square opposite north gate of Beihai Park
Nightly impromptu ballroom dancing right by the lake.

Yueli Yuan Flower Garden
Ditan Park
Open daily 7–10pm, April to mid-October.

Bars and Pubs
Chaoyang Park West Gate
Nongzhanguan Lu
Goose and Duck and Suzie Wong's draw expats and the women who 'love' them; Souk is one of Beijing's best hangouts with Middle Eastern food and great cocktails.

Frank's Place
Gongti Donglu, Chaoyang
Tel: 10-6507 2617
All-American and UK watering hole draws the older expat set with good food, beers and big-screen sports. Open 9am–midnight.

Hou Hai
Qianhai, Houhai, opposite north gate o[f] Beihai Park
Lotus Lane is a brand new strip of upscal[e] bars, other indistinguishables line the tw[o] lakes and the surrounding alleys. No Nam[e] Bar, at the Yinding Bridge is one of th[e] models, Lotus (on Yandaixie Jie) is yin t[o] Huxley's 'shut up and drink' yang.

Passby Bar
108 Nanluogu Xiang
Tel: 10-6401 9474
Marvelous courtyard bar-restaurant with [a] library, lovely décor and ambience in a[n] historic *hutong* (alley) southeast of the Dru[m] and Bell Towers. Open daily 11am–2pm.

Women's Street 'Super Bar Street'
Nuren Jie, Dongfang Qicai Shijie, opposit[e] the Israeli embassy
Sitting on a north-side patio (like Jean's[)] you don't realize you're seeing a filthy pond[.] Get Lucky is Beijing's rock (and, upstairs[)] 'full-service' karaoke) palace with home[-] brewed beer. Pula Pula is where the kids g[o] to shake their groove things.

Wudaokou
Line 13 subway stop; between Qinghua[University and Beijing Language Institute[,] on Xueyuan Lu, Haidian District
Where the foreign student contingent and [a] minority of brave locals go to unwind wit[h] cheap drinks. Propaganda is a dance club[.] Lush features open-mic Sundays.

Discos
Mix and Vics
North gate of Workers' Stadium
Tel: 10-6530 2889; 6593 6215
Two clubs opposite one another draw steady crowds with pop-hip hop, RnB and dance music. Vics is for the younger – often too younger – crowd. Open nightly from 8pm.

Nightman
2 Xibahenanli, Chaoyang
Tel: 10-6466 2522
Young Chinese and Westerners dance non-stop to hip-hop, house, techno. Now somewhat rundown and out of fashion. Free entry for foreigners. Open daily 8pm–3am.

Rock N' Roll
Yard 4, Gongti Beilu, behind the Comfort Inn
Tel: 10-6592 9856
The massive complex, which was recently relocated, is packed with Beijingers gyrating to the latest disco tunes. Open daily 8pm–5am.

Success
4 Gongti Beilu (opposite Yaxiu Market)
Tel: 10-6595 9494 ext 8006
This is the ultimate Beijing kitsch experience, and comes complete with go-go dancers, cabaret, KTV and more. Open daily from 8pm.

Tango
South gate of Ditan Park
Tel: 10-6428 2288
This is a super-sized disco, live venue, lounge bar, karaoke all located under one roof. Open daily, 24 hours.

The Den
4A Gongti Donglu, next to the City Hotel
Tel: 10-6592 6290
Restaurant-cum-disco, with a good brunch for the morning after. Seventies and eighties dance music is played upstairs. The place is popular with young Chinese women and older expats, and fills up around midnight. Open daily 1pm–3am.

Above: Chaoyang acrobats

Cinema
Cherry Lane Movies
An Jia Lou, inside Kent Centre, 70m north of Liangmaqiao Lu
Tel: 139-0113 4745
www.cherrylanemovies.com.cn
Chinese films with English subtitles shown, every Friday and Saturday night at 8pm. The theatre's occasional guests include directors and scholars.

Traditional Theatre and Shows
China Puppet Theatre
1 Anhua Xili
Tel: 10-6425 4849, 6425 4798
Traditional stories acted out by shadow- and hand-puppets. Performances on Sat and Sun only, 9.30–10.30am; 10.30–11.50am.

Lao She Teahouse
3/F, 3 Qianmenxi Dajie, Qianmen
Tel: 10-6303 6830
Nightly performances (7.50–9.20pm) include excerpts from Peking opera, acrobatics, magic and comedy.

Liyuan Theatre
175 Yongan Lu, Jianguo Hotel Qianmen
Tel: 10-6301 6688 ext 8860
Popular Peking opera venue. Performances daily 7.30–8.45pm.

Sanwei Bookstore
60 Fuxingmennei Dajie, Xicheng
Tel: 10-6601 3204
Traditional teahouse above bookshop. Friday is jazz night, Saturday is Chinese classical music. Open daily 9.30am–10.30pm.

Wan Sheng Theatre
Tianqiao (to the west of the Temple of Heaven)
Tel: 10-6303 7449
Popular acrobatics performances by a local acrobatics troupe are held daily at 5.30pm and 7.15pm.

Zhengyici Theatre
220 Xiheyan Dajie, Hepingmen Wai, Zhengyici, Juchang
Tel: 10-8315 1649
Renovations will be completed by 2006; at the time of press, plans for this opera venue were unclear.

CALENDAR OF EVENTS

Whenever you arrive in China, it will be close to an official holiday or traditional festival. Holidays such as National Day (1 October) and International Labour Day (1 May) are fixed, but traditional festivals are set according to the lunar calendar and so vary from year to year. Dates for these celebrations, and information on annual events like the Beijing Marathon, can be obtained through the Beijing branch of the China International Travel Service (CITS) (Tourism Building, 28 Jianguomenwai Dajie; tel: 10-6515 8264).

January/February

The new calendar year begins with the tolling of the bell at the Big Bell Temple (Dazhongsi) and a one-day public holiday. The western new year is growing in popularity, with TV specials and parties at the Great Wall. But the biggest bash remains the lunar new year, known as **Spring Festival** or, in the West, as **Chinese New Year**. It normally starts in late January or early February. The date varies because it is traditionally set so that it falls on the second new moon after the winter solstice. Every December and January, public buildings are festooned with lights and banners. People across China travel to see their families, debts are settled, and the making and buying of food and drink builds toward its frenetic climax. In northern China, a holiday staple is boiled *jiaozi* (pasta parcels similar to ravioli). Both eating *jiaozi* and gathering family and friends to help with the time-consuming process of making them are important Spring Festival traditions. At midnight on the eve of the Spring Festival, firecrackers still sound across the city (in defiance of a ban) and there are large pub-

lic fireworks displays. On the first day of the lunar year, people don their best clothes and go out to visit friends and relatives. Traditionally, everyone, no matter how poor, must put on new clothes to usher in good luck in the new year. In recent years, a more relaxed atmosphere has seen the return of old traditions such as giving *hongbao* (little red envelopes containing money) to children. Beijing's 'little emperors' (pampered children), now usually expect at least 50 yuan. Throughout the Spring Festival week, temple fairs at Longtan Park and Ditan Park feature folk dancing, opera, martial arts, comedy, food and toy stalls. The fairs at Taoist Baiyunguan, Tibetan-Buddhist Yonghegong and other temples are mainly religious and are very popular among locals. Travelling during this period is a nightmarish experience.

Beijingers, who have an amazing resilience to the bitter winters, relish ice-skating, sledding and winter swimming. Many lakes and canals, including Kunming Lake at the Summer Palace and the moat of the Imperial Palace, are used as skating rinks. Throughout the winter, Longqing Gorge outside Beijing holds its **Ice Lantern Festival**.

March/April

March brings a breather for Chinese women. **International Women's Day** on 8 March is an official holiday for those who 'hold up (more than) half the sky'.

On the 12th day of the third lunar month people honour their dead relatives by observing **Qingming**, or 'grave-sweeping' day.

With spring comes the **Beijing International Kite Festival** at the Mentougou Sports Centre, staged for five days in mid-April. Beijing's leading kite-makers show off their elaborate dragon kites alongside hi-tech stunt kites from abroad. The tradition of kite-flying dates back at least 2,500 years in China.

In late April and early May, the Beijing Botanical Gardens, close to Fragrant Hills Park, bursts into a riot of colours for the **Peach Blossom Festival**.

May/June

International Labour Day is a one-day public holiday, much more low-key since the economic reforms, with no more massive military parades. Following hot on its heels is

Above: a Spring Festival fair

Youth Day, a commemoration of the May Fourth Movement of 1919, reflected mainly by editorials and government support in the Chinese media. However, since 2000, the official holiday period starting from 1 May is seven days long. The domestic tourist industry literally takes off, so if you are planning to travel during these days, plan in advance.

International Children's Day is celebrated in earnest on 1 June, by letting out classes early and treating children to outings to a park or zoo.

The crushing of the Tiananmen Square protests on 4 June 1989 is not, of course, officially marked, but it is not forgotten either. Extra uniformed and plain-clothes police officers are stationed around the city.

To beat the dog days of summer, a new **Water Melon Festival** takes place in Daxing county, outside Beijing, at the end of June, right up to the first week of July.

July/August

1 July is the **Anniversary of the Founding of the Communist Party**, which began in Shanghai in 1921. Celebrations include banquets held for important party members.

The fifth day of the fifth lunar month, usually late July, brings the **Dragon Boat Festival**, marked in Beijing by international dragon boat races. The festival has been celebrated since China's earliest times and a number of legends are associated with it. Triangular *zongzi*, sticky rice cakes wrapped in bamboo leaves, used to be thrown into the river where a famous poet is said to have hurled himself overboard. Today, *zongzi* are eaten to mark the occasion. The location of the boat races change each year. Check tourist publications or your hotel information desk.

From late July through early September, Beijing celebrates the **Lantern Festival** in Beihai and other parks. The festival dates back 3,000 years and is believed to be connected with the lifting of evening curfew for a few days at this time of year. Elaborate home-made lanterns light up the streets.

1 August is the **Anniversary of the People's Liberation Army**. The date can be seen in Chinese characters on army caps and collar badges. Inaugurated in 1927 and once marked by enormous parades, it is now played out mainly in the official media.

Right: Longqing Ice Lantern Festival

September/October

The **Mid-Autumn Festival** again depends on when the moon reaches its fullest, usually around mid-September. Shops do a roaring trade in 'moon' cakes, round pastries filled with combinations of sesame paste, nuts, red beans, dried fruit, etc.

Late September is normally when the Chinese celebrate the memory of Confucius. Beijing's Temple of Confucius (Kong Miao) has revived the annual ceremony. As Confucius is China's most famous teacher, the event has been combined with **Teachers' Day**.

1 October is the birthday of the People's Republic of China (PRC). **National Day** was formerly celebrated with a two-day public holiday but since 1999 the holiday is seven days. Again, plan in advance if you are intending to travel during this period. Five- and 10-year anniversaries have been accompanied by grandiose fireworks exhibitions and performances by dancers in Tiananmen Square. In other years, government buildings, road junctions and hotels are decked out in lights and flower arrangements. In the third week of October, when the weather is almost always glorious, the city hosts the **Beijing International Marathon**.

November/December

These are quiet, cold months in northern China, but **Christmas** is gaining momentum as a celebration for both consumers, Christians and curious onlookers. It is now trendy to exchange Christmas cards and gifts, while in shopping areas, Santa makes the odd appearance. Most large hotels have special meals and events promotions. Even small restaurants now put up Christmas decorations, which often remain in place until after Spring Festival the following year.

Practical Information

GETTING THERE

By Air

Beijing's Capital Airport, 30km (18 miles) from the centre, connects the city to all parts of China and to the world's major cities. The airport has a new terminal building. For airport enquiries, call tel: 10-6512 8931 or www.caft.com.

Capital Airport has connections to most other cities in China. You must check in at least 30 minutes before departure for a domestic flight and at least one hour before departure for an international flight. For shorter journeys within China, the train is often a better bet. The airport tax is now included in the ticket price.

Taxis are on the left as you leave the terminal. Don't ride with the touts in the terminal offering taxis and make sure the taxi driver uses the meter. The journey to the city centre takes 30 minutes if the traffic is light, but can take an hour at busier times. You will have to pay the highway toll (10 yuan). Express bus routes run to various parts of Beijing, one to the Beijing International Hotel (north of Beijing Train Station) while CACC (Civil Aviation Administration of China) runs buses to its main office in Xidan (west of Tiananmen Square). Larger hotels provide shuttle buses from the airport.

Domestic Airlines

China's national tourist offices and travel agencies, including hotel travel desks, can give you the current flight schedule of domestic airlines. You can buy tickets from travel agencies or airline booking offices. Travel agencies may be more convenient: although they charge more, they are more likely to have English speaking staff. Try Fesco Air Services, 1st Floor, China World Trade Centre; tel: 10-6505 3330. Otherwise, try China International Travel Services (CITS) (tel: 10-8522 8888; www.cits.com.cn) (*see page 89*).

By Rail

Beijing has two main railway stations: Beijing Station (Beijing Zhan) and Beijing West (Xi Zhan). Some trains to other parts of China run from the city's three smaller stations. Trans-Siberian trains leave from Beijing Station, the start of a fascinating five-day (via Mongolia) or six-day (via Northeast China) journey to Moscow. The Beijing International Hotel (9 Jianguomennei Dajie; tel: 10-6512 0507) has an international train ticket booking office.

If you are arriving on the Trans-Siberian, the same health and customs procedures apply as for international arrivals by air. Taxis are plentiful at Beijing Station and the same rules apply as at the airport. Less expensive, although usually very crowded, are buses which will take you downtown for only 2 yuan; there is also a subway stop at the station.

For travel within China, the best place to buy tickets is the foreigners' booking office to the left of the main concourse inside Beijing Station, where you can also buy tickets for trains leaving from Beijing West Station. Beijing West also has a foreigners' booking office. If you want a sleeper berth, especially in summer, buy your ticket at least five days in advance. Return tickets can be purchased for Hong Kong–Beijing, but not other routes.

By Road

Long-distance buses connect Beijing with many cities. These include Tianjin, Chengde, Beidaihe and Taiyuan. On some routes taking the bus is faster, but generally less comfortable, than trains. The sleeper buses operate on longer routes. Buses are recom-

Left: well-organised bicycle park
Right: Beijing is well-connected by air

mended for shorter journeys, to places like Tianjin (two hours) or Chengde (four hours). Beijing's main long-distance bus stations are at Dongzhimen, Xizhimen and Yongdingmen.

TRAVEL ESSENTIALS

When to Visit

The best time to visit Beijing is from early September through to late November, when it's normally dry and sunny, with moderate temperatures. If you visit between March and May, chances are you'll encounter at least one of the annual dust storms that blow off the Gobi Desert. Summers are hot, with occasional torrential downpours. The hottest month, July, averages 26°C (79°F) but temperatures occasionally soar to nearly 40°C (104°F). Beijing winters are cold but mostly sunny. The coldest month, January, averages about -5°C (23°F), but temperatures can drop to as low as -23°C (-9°F). Locals wear several layers of clothing all winter, but fear not – one of the best buys in China is silk thermal underwear.

Visas and Passports

Valid passports and visas are required for all foreign tourists. Visas may be obtained at embassies or consulates of the People's Republic of China, or through overseas offices of the state-run China International Travel Service.

Most group tourists are allowed entry through group visas. For individual travellers, single-entry visas are valid for entry within three months of issue. Visas are usually issued for 30 to 60 days, and can be extended for another 30 days in China for a small fee at the foreign affairs section of Public Security Bureau at Andingmen Dongdajie, just east of the Lamma Temple, tel: 10-6404 7799.

Business or study visas are issued on presentation of a letter or similar official document from any recognised Chinese organisation. Business travellers can be issued with multi-entry visas that are valid for six months to one year.

Carry your passport with you at all times, as it will often be required for checking into hotels, making reservations, changing money, and for bank transactions. If your passport is lost or stolen, contact your embassy immediately, and also the Public Security Bureau.

Customs

Written declarations are required only for visitors carrying more than US$5,000, or who exceed duty-free limits. Chinese customs are especially sensitive to pornographic material as well as publications deemed to be anti-government. Antiques dating from prior to 1795 cannot legally be taken out of the country *(see page 66)*. Foreigners carrying illicit drugs have been sentenced to long prison terms.

Electricity

Electrical current runs at 220 volts. Many hotels have 110-volt shaver sockets.

Time

Beijing time is eight hours ahead of Greenwich Mean Time (GMT).

GETTING ACQUAINTED

Geography

Beijing municipality covers 16,808 sq km (6,488 sq miles). To its south is the fertile North China Plain and to the east, the Bohai Sea. To the west, northwest and northeast are mountain ranges.

Government and Economy

Beijing is the capital of the People's Republic of China; Hu Jintao is General Secretary of the Communist Party of China (CPC), president of the country, and, as of September 2004, the Chairman of the CPC control Military Commission. Wen Jiabao is China's Premier. The 3,000-strong legislative body, the National People's Congress (NPC) meets annually in Beijing. In theory, the NPC can approve or reject legislation, but it is widely regarded as a rubber-stamp parliament. Real power lies with the nine members of the Standing Committee of the CCP Politburo (sometimes known as China's cabinet). But personal connections and bureaucracy remain key features of day-to-day government and civil service operations.

Right: locals relax in Tiananmen Square

Beijing is one of four municipalities (along with Shanghai, Tianjin and, since 1997, Chongqing) with status equal to that of China's provinces. It is divided into 10 separate administrative districts. The city's local government set-up mirrors that of the central government; it is led by the Communist Party with limited participation by non-party officials.

China's economy is in transition from socialism to a 'socialist market economy'. Beijing is still behind many southern and coastal cities in encouraging capitalism. The city is striving to catch up by modelling itself on Singapore. Places such as banks and post offices are still in the grip of the old system, but the new system is especially evident in the huge number of privately run restaurants and retail outlets.

Religion

For most of the period of Communist rule since 1949, worship of all kinds was discouraged or actively suppressed. Since 1978, the main religions have been allowed to revive, but most urban Chinese are atheists. Buddhism, Taoism, Islam and Christianity are all practised in temples, mosques and churches around Beijing.

Evangelising outside these institutions is forbidden and all religious groups are supposed to register with the government. Even so, Beijing has some underground (ie unregistered) Christian groups.

Population

Beijing has a population of almost 14.5 million, making it China's second-largest city after Shanghai (13.5 million). The majority Han people make up about 97 percent of the population. Of the 300,000 minority people in the city, about half are Muslims. As many as three million migrant workers from other parts of the country and around 100,000 foreigners live in Beijing.

MONEY MATTERS

Currency

The Chinese currency is the renminbi (RMB or 'people's currency') yuan. Hotel rates are often cited in US dollars, but can be paid in renminbi. Foreign currency can be exchanged for renminbi at banks, the Friendship Store and some big shopping centres.

When you change money, you get a receipt that allows you to change renminbi back to foreign currency within six months. However, you can only change back up to 50 percent of the original sum.

Chinese money is counted in yuan, jiao and fen. One yuan is 100 fen or 10 jiao; one jiao is 10 fen. Colloquially, a yuan is usually called a kuai and a jiao is called a mao. Bills are denominated in 1, 2 and 5 jiao, and 1, 2, 5, 10, 20, 50 and 100 yuan. There are also 1 yuan, 5 jiao and 1 jiao coins, plus almost worthless 1, 2 and 5 fen coins.

Credit Cards

Major credit and charge cards like Diner's Club, Federal Card, American Express, MasterCard, Visa and JCB are accepted at all but low-budget hotels. Some restaurants and stores geared toward tourism also accept them, and a small, albeit growing, number of ATMs (Cirrus, Plus, Star, Visa, Mastercard, etc) can be used for withdrawing cash.

Money Changers

Since Chinese *renminbi* is not fully convertible to foreign currency, there is a small black market for foreign currency.

The main reason why the black market still persists is because it is technically illegal for most Chinese businesses to conduct foreign currency transactions, so they obtain foreign currency through illegal channels.

The black market exchange rates are little more than those in banks and hotels, so changing money illegally on the street is no longer worth the hassle, or the risk of being cheated or even arrested (the latter is unlikely, but you could be the unlucky victim of a sudden police crackdown).

If you do choose to change money on the black market, avoid money-changers who try to rush you, who ask you to walk into a back street with them, or who are not obviously connected with a store. These people are often very good at sleight of hand. The 'safest' places to change money illegally are at the stores and market stalls.

Price Differences

In 1996, China officially abolished the practice of charging foreigners higher prices for hotels, entrance to tourist sites and so on. Most places have complied, resulting in large price rises for Chinese visitors. But vendors at markets, food stands and privately-run restaurants often try to charge foreigners more, as in many countries. The best way to deal with this is to find out local prices as soon as possible and insist on paying them, or walk away. If you are unsure of prices in a restaurant, find out the prices of individual dishes before ordering them.

Tipping

In Chairman Mao's time, tipping was thought of as a bourgeois affectation. For better or worse, some hotel staff have come to expect tips, especially bell boys and restroom attendants. Taxi drivers and door attendants do not expect tips. Restaurants catering to foreigners usually add a 10 or 15 percent service charge to the bill.

GETTING AROUND

Taxis

Beijing is oversupplied with taxis, which are inexpensive and convenient. Smaller cars cost 1.20 or 1.60 yuan per kilometre. Larger cars cost 2 yuan per kilometre. Always make sure the metre is switched on before setting off. A few taxi drivers speak English but it is a good idea to carry the name and address of your hotel (name cards in Chinese are very useful for this) and ensure that your destination is written in Chinese before setting off. Drivers must post their car number and identity card inside the taxi, so you can note down these details in case of complaints. While taxi drivers must attend English classes once a week (as the city prepares for the 2008 Olympics), the English ability of most drivers is currently non-existent.

Beijing's taxi drivers are generally honest. Do not assume the worst if they take convoluted routes. The city's many one-way streets and complex traffic rules forbid left turns at many junctions. But drivers who line up for hours in front of hotels are often hoping for big fares.

Taxis can also be rented for longer trips, such as whole-day tours or visits to the Great Wall or Ming Tombs. If you plan to do this, make sure you agree to the total fare and the precise itinerary in advance. Call

Left: taxis display signs denoting cost
Top right: busy subway station

Beijing Taxi (tel: 10-6837 3399); or simply ask a cabbie you have come to like.

Bus

Beijing's intricate and changing bus network can be a mystery even to lifelong residents of the city. Buses are slow and crowded and the distances between stops are sometimes long; on the other hand, they are a very inexpensive means of transport. A few routes have now been improved, with air-conditioned double-decker buses plying them. Minibuses use the same routes as the buses, and although they offer a faster, more comfortable service at several times the ordinary bus fare, these prices are still low by Western standards.

Subway

The city's subway system is being expanded for the 2008 Olympics but at present it consists of just three lines. It provides a useful link to tourist sights such as Tiananmen Square, the Lama Temple and shopping areas like Wangfujing. It gets crowded during rush hour, though it is preferable to the bus. Recordings in English and Chinese announce the stops. Buy your ticket (3–5 yuan) when you enter the subway station.

Cars

Hire cars come with drivers and can be hired from most hotels. Negotiate for half- and whole-day rates. Foreign tourists are not allowed to drive in China, unless given special permission.

Try the following companies: Beijing Limo (tel: 130-3105 2512); Beijing Capital Auto Group (tel: 10-6775 0039); or Today New Concept Car Rental (tel: 10-6457 5566).

Bicycles

Cycling is the most enjoyable way to see hill-less Beijing, but it requires steady nerves and basic fitness. If you are not used to urban cycling, it is a good idea to get some practice before going to China.

Many hotels have bicycles for hire; if your hotel cannot rent you one, they can advise

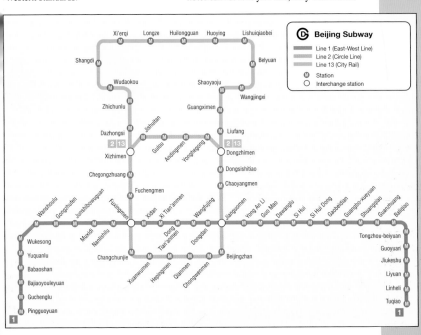

you where to go. Budget hotels typically rent out bikes for around 10 yuan per day (plus deposit); more upmarket hotels charge in excess of 100 yuan per day or 35 yuan per hour (plus deposit). Shops around Qianhou Hai also rent single and two-person bikes. Beijingers ride all year round, through all kinds of weather, even on snow or ice.

Pedicabs

If you want to experience travelling through Beijing at a cyclist's pace but don't feel up to cycling yourself, pedicabs – three-wheeled bicycles that accommodate up to two passengers at the back plus the driver in front – can be hired near many tourist sites (especially Qian Houhai and Qianmen) and larger hotels. Some hotels have their own pedicabs at set prices. Prices are negotiable from 5 to 30 yuan, depending on the distance you wish to go and the time of day. A ride from the Friendship Store to Tiananmen Square, about 4km (2½ miles), will cost you around 20 yuan, for example.

You'll find that pedicabs are often more expensive than taxis, but as Beijing's rush hour traffic jams worsen by the day, it can sometimes be faster to walk, cycle or hop into a pedicab rather than take a taxi to a nearby destination.

If you are interested in taking a pedicab tour of Beijing's *hutong* (alleys), you can arrange this in advance with the Hutong Pedicab Company. The company is located at 26 Dianmen Nei Xidajie; tel: 10-6612 3236 or simply head to the Qian Hou Hai or Dazhalan areas.

HOURS AND HOLIDAYS

Business Hours

Business hours vary. Government offices, including banks, are generally open 8am–5pm. Some close earlier and most have a lunch break from noon–1pm. Offices also open on Saturday mornings, but not on Sundays. The best time to get things done is at the start of the working day.

Most shops open at 9am and close around 9pm, though if they are still state run they can close by 6pm. Many department stores and privately run small stores open until 9pm. Money exchange outlets – but not banks – are open seven days a week and also generally operate long hours. At the tourist sites, ticket sales may stop 30 minutes before closing time and many museums are closed on Mondays.

ACCOMMODATION

Luxury hotels abound in Beijing, while the construction of many more is in progress, in anticipation of the Beijing Olympics in 2008. There are few bargains, and this is mainly due to the state-set minimums on room rates. Hotels marked JV indicate that these are joint ventures run by foreign management, which often means they offer better service at higher cost. Rates at all but the budget hotels are subject to 10–15 percent tax and service charges. The published hotel rates for a standard double room are categorised as follows:

$$$$ = US$200 and up;
$$$ = US$150–200;
$$ = US$100–150;
$ = US$50–100

Beijing
$$$$

Beijing Hotel
33 Dongchang'an Jie, Dongcheng
Tel: 10-6513 7766
Fax: 10-6513 7842
e-mail: business@chinabeijinghotel.com.cn
Opened in 1917 and recently refurbished, with a long list of famous guests. Period features give it an air of tradition, in contrast to many newer competitors. Centrally located, on the corner of Wangfujing shopping street.

China World Hotel
1 Jianguomenwai Dajie, Chaoyang East
Tel: 10-6505 2266
Fax: 10-6505 0828
www.shangri-la.com
Top class service and accommodations, with health club, swimming pool, shopping and business centres, plus several Western and Asian restaurants. It is well located for business travellers.

Right: the Beijing Hotel

Grand Hyatt Beijing
1 Dongchang'an Jie, Dongcheng
Tel: 10-8518 1234
Fax: 10-8518 0000
www.beijing.grand.hyatt.com
First-rate hotel ensconced in the impressive Oriental Plaza complex. Beijing's premier shopping street, Wangfujing Dajie, is next door and the Forbidden City a stroll away. Excellent choice of restaurants.

Holiday Inn Crowne Plaza
48 Wangfujing Dajie, Dengshikou,
Dongcheng
Tel: 10-6513 3388
Fax: 10-6513 2513
www.crowneplaza.com
email: hicpb@public3.bta.net.cn
Also in Wangfujing, the hotel has its own gallery of modern Chinese art and a salon for performances of traditional Chinese music.

The Peninsula Palace
8 Jinyu Hutong, Wangfujing Dajie,
Dongcheng
Tel: 10-8516 2888
Fax: 10-6510 6311
Modern, functional hotel with Chinese imperial flourishes. A waterfall cascades down into a lobby full of Chinese antiques, while designer labels compete in the shopping arcade.

St Regis
21 Jianguomenwai Dajie, Dongcheng
Tel: 10-6460 6688
Fax: 10-6460 3299
A marvellous and centrally-located five-star hotel with a supremely elegant foyer, fine restaurants and a high standard of luxury. The hotel's Press Club Bar is a favourite of the expat business community.

$$$
Gloria Plaza Hotel
2 Jianguomen Nandajie, Chaoyang East
Tel: 10-6515 8855
Fax: 10-6515 8533
www.hotel-web.com/gloria/beijing
With a great location on a major junction, opposite the Ancient Observatory and next to one of the main CITS offices, the Gloria Plaza has several restaurants and an American-style sports bar.

Kempinski Hotel
50 Liangmaqiao Lu, Beijing Lufthansa
Centre, Chaoyang Northeast
Tel: 10-6465 3388
Fax: 10-6465 3366
www.kempinski_beijing.com
email: khblc.public.east.cn.net
Attached to Friendship (Youyi) Shopping City, this hotel has all the facilities a discerning traveller could ask for, including a health club, restaurants and the authentic German Paulaner Brauhaus restaurant and pub.

Lee Garden Service Apartments
18 Jinyu Hutong Wangfujing
Tel: 6525-8855
Fax: 6525-7999
e-mail:
general.manager@lgapartment.com
Good option for long-term stays or for those who like to have their own kitchen and other comforts of home. The suites range in size from studio to three-room, all with kitchen

Well located at the northern end of the China World Trade Centre business complex. With solid service, food and accommodations, this is a less expensive option than the neighbouring China World Hotel.

$$

Beijing International Hotel
19 Jianguomenwai Dajie, Dongcheng
Tel: 10-6512 6688
Fax: 10-6512 9972
With a good location near Beijing Railway Station and the Henderson and Cofco Plaza shopping centres, this 1,000-room hotel offers a full range of facilities, including a booking offices for international flights and trains.

Dragon Spring Hotel
Shuizha Beilu, Mentougou
Tel: 10-6984 3366/3362
Fax: 10-6984 4377
For atmosphere and facilities, this international hotel, built in classical Chinese style, beats most similarly priced hotels in the city. The only disadvantage is that it is located near the Western Hills, about an hour from the city centre.

Fragrant Hills Hotel
inside Fragrant Hills Park
Tel: 10-6259 1166
Fax: 10-6259 1762
A modern sanctuary for respite from the urban hustle and bustle, in the lush hills northwest of Beijing, beyond the Summer Palace. There is a swimming pool and both Chinese and Western restaurants.

Friendship Hotel
3 Baishiqiao Lu, Haidian
Tel: 10-6849 8888
Fax: 10-6849 8866
www.cbw.com/hotel/friendship
Part of a huge, state-run hotel spread out in pleasant grounds close to the Summer Palace and university district, the hotel has several sections offering a range of prices and facilities. It is also home to many foreigners working for Chinese state employers.

Jing Guang New World Hotel
Hujia Lou, Dongsanhuan Lu,
Chaoyang East

and full bath. This 199-room hotel offers the usual luxury hotel facilities, plus childcare and a children's play area. Some rooms have balconies with a view of the Forbidden City.

Red Capital Club Residence
9 Dongsi Liutiao, Dongcheng
Tel: 10-8403 5308
Fax: 10-6402 7153
www.redcapitalclub.com.cn
A boutique hotel in a renovated courtyard that is companion to the restaurant 3 *hutongs* north. Sip wine in a former bomb shelter beneath the hotel's 5 suites.

State Guest Hotel
9 Fuchengmenwai Road, Xicheng District
Tel: 6800-5588
Fax: 6800-5888
www.stateguesthotel.com
A modern addition to the Diaoyutai State Guest House, the State Guest Hotel has less stringent security and more modern facilities. All 502 rooms have high-speed internet access and multiple phone lines. Guests can relax or socialise in the four-storey atrium lobby.

Traders' Hotel
1 Jianguomenwai Dajie, Chaoyang East
Tel: 10-6505 2277
Fax: 10-6505 0818
www.shangri-la.com

Above: lobby, Holiday Inn Crowne Plaza
Right: bar at the Kempinski Hotel

Tel: 10-6597 8888
Fax: 10-6597 3333
A 53-storey building dominating the eastern Third Ring Road, the Jing Guang New World is almost a self-contained town, with its own bakery, restaurants, nightclubs, children's play areas, medical centre and supermarket – and, of course, some of the best views of Beijing.

Novotel Peace Hotel
3 Jinyu Hutong, Dongcheng
Tel: 10-6512 8833
Fax: 10-6512 6863
On the other side of the road from the Palace Hotel, the Novotel Peace is a smart and modern four-star hotel with a central location just off Wangfujing Dajie.

Shangri-La Hotel
29 Zizhuyuan Lu, Haidian
Tel: 10-6841 2211
Fax: 10-6841 8004
www.shangri-la.com
This tasteful high-rise hotel has meeting rooms, a ballroom, French and Asian restaurants and a full range of other facilities. On the western edge of the city, it provides a shuttle-bus service to downtown areas.

Zijin Guesthouse
9 Chongwenmen Xidajie, Dongcheng
Tel/Fax: 10-6513 6655 ext. 3800
Located in the former Belgian Legation in the Foreign Legation Quarter (see itinerary

5), this comfortable hotel is in an excellent position for reaching both Tiananmen Square and Wangfujing Dajie. The reception is in building No 7 in the northeast corner of the compound.

$
Beijing Backpackers Hostel
85 Nan Luoguxiang, Dongcheng
Tel: 10-8400 2429
www.backpackingchina.com
Brand new hostel in the hutongs of Jiaodaokou. Spitting distance from Grant Cafés like Passby, and walking distance to Houhai.

Beijing Bamboo Garden Hotel
24 Xiaoshiqiao Hutong, Jiugulou Dajie
Tel: 10-6403 2229
Fax: 10-6401 2633
Simple, clean rooms open onto a classical Chinese garden, close to the Drum Tower. What it lacks in facilities compared with large, modern hotels, it more than compensates for in atmosphere.

Fangyuan Hotel
36 Dengshikou Xijie, Dongcheng
Tel: 10-6525 6331
Fax: 10-6513 8549
The two-star Fangyuan Hotel may not be particularly smart, but the location just off Wangfujing Dajie and opposite the former home of Lao She (an important 20th-century writer), plus its range of inexpensive

rooms, make this worth considering. Breakfast is included.

Haoyuan Hotel
Shijia Hutong, Dongsinan Dajie,
Dongcheng
Tel: 10-6512 5557
Fax: 10-6525 3179
Hidden away in a narrow alley near the busy Dongdan shopping street and close to the Palace Hotel, the Haoyuan's rooms surround two quiet courtyards. The buildings are a traditional combination of brick and red lacquered wood, with curved tiles on the roofs. A small restaurant serves hearty traditional fare at very reasonable prices.

Lusongyuan Hotel
22 Banchang Hutong, Kuanjie, Dongcheng
Tel: 10-6401 1116
Fax: 10-6403 0418
This courtyard hotel was established in 1980 in the residence of a former Qing dynasty official. The rooms are refined and airy. Stone lions still guard the traditional wooden gate, which leads to the pavilions, trees, rockeries and potted plants that fill the courtyards. Great location in the Jiaedaokou *hutongs*

Outside Beijing
$$
Chengde
Qiwanglou Hotel
1 Bifengmen Lu
Tel: 0314-202 4385
For atmosphere alone, this establishment is the best option you can find in Chengde. The small, exquisitely refurbished hotel occupies a Qing dynasty mansion, which is set just inside the grounds of the imperial resort.
$$

Yunshan Hotel
2 Bandishan Lu
Tel: 0314-205 5588
This is the main tourist hotel in Chengde, close to the station and with some of the best facilities.

$
Mongolian Yurt Holiday Village
Tel: 0314-216 3094
Economical and kitsch *yurts* (containing TVs, washrooms and air-conditioning) are available within the grounds of the imperial resort.

Mountain Villa Hotel
11 Lizhetngmen Dajie
Tel: 0314-202 3501
This good-value hotel is well positioned opposite the imperial resort and has a variety of restaurants.

Beidaihe/Shanhaiguan
$$
Beidaihe Guesthouse for Diplomatic Missions
1 Baosan Lu, Beidaihe
Tel: 0335-404 1287
Standing just five minutes away from the main beach, this hotel has friendly staff and a good seafood restaurant. All the rooms have balconies with fine sea views. Open Apr–Oct.

$
Jiaohai Hotel
97 Dongjing Lu
Tel: 0335-404 1388
Fax: 0335-404 1388
This modern and clean three-star hotel has

Above: Gloria Plaza Hotel

swimming pool and is just a short walk way from the beachfront. **$**

Jingshan Hotel
Dong Dajie, Shanhaiguan
Tel: 0335-505 1130
Next to the famous East Gate of the Shanhaiguan garrison on the Great Wall, the Jingshan has comfortable rooms in the heart of the small town. **$**

HEALTH AND EMERGENCIES

Hygiene/General Health
Tap water should always be boiled before drinking. Some hotels have water purifaction systems and they all sell bottled water and provide flasks of boiled water in guests' rooms. Brushing teeth with tap water is not a problem. Bottled water and canned soft drinks are available at tourist sites and sold on most streets.

Although they are not necessarily unsafe, avoid ice cream, yoghurt and drinks from large vats. If buying food from street vendors, make sure it is piping hot and freshly cooked and served in clean dishes, preferably disposable ones. Don't patronise restaurants with dirty utensils or poor food-handling practices, to avoid contracting hepatitis, which is endemic. And wash your hands frequently. Except in the hotels, most toilets are the crude though renovated squat type. Carry your own toilet paper.

Colds and stomach disorders are the most common travellers' complaints. Attention to hygiene goes a long way towards preventing both. Medicines that may come in handy are Panadol, Lomotil (or Imodium), general antibiotics, Pepto-Bismol and aspirin. Watson with outlets all over the city, has a wide selection of Western medicines. Malaria prevention medication is not necessary for Beijing or anywhere in northern China.

Consult your doctor or a travel clinic nurse for recommended vaccinations (eg Hepatitis A) before travelling to China. In the UK, MASTA (Medical Advisory Service for Travellers Abroad) can provide up-to-date information (tel: 0906 8 224 100) on all medical matters.

Medical Services
In case of dire emergency, dial 120 for an ambulance; or Beijing International SOS Clinic (5 Sanliton Xiwujie; tel: 10-6462 9112; 24-hour alarm tel: 10-6462 9100). Two of the best hospitals for foreigners are the Sino-Japanese Friendship Hospital (north end of Heping Lu; tel: 10-6422 2952) and the Peking Union Medical Hospital (53 Dongdanbei Dajie; emergency tel: 10-6529 5284). The Beijing International Medical Center (Room 106 Regus Office Building, Lufthansa Centre; tel: 10-6465 1561, 6465 1562) is an outpatient clinic geared to foreigners.

COMMUNICATIONS AND NEWS

Mail
Hotel desks provide the most convenient service for posting letters and parcels. The International Post Office (open 8am–6.30pm; tel: 10-6512-8114) on Yabao Lu, about 300m (330yds) north of the Jianguomen junction, handles international mail and is Beijing's *poste restante* address.

Telephone
Major hotels have IDD service available in the rooms, and smaller hotels usually have business centres with IDD. In shopping areas there are phonecard booths: cards are normally available in 20, 50, 100 and 200 yuan units. The cheapest way to call abroad is to buy an IP (Internet Phone) card, available from newspaper kiosks and hotels.

US credit phone card access codes from China are as follows. Sprint tel: 108-16; AT&T tel: 108-888; MCI/Worldphone tel: 108-712. Fax, cable, e-mail and Internet services are also widely available in hotels.

Cell phone coverage in China is good. With upwards of 5.5 million new mobile phone subscribers in China every month, it would have to be. China Unicom has agreements with 13 mobile operators from around the world, so there is a good chance that your dual- or tri-band phone will work on 'roam' in Beijing. Alternatively, buy local SIM cards (with a local number) for 100 yuan in one of the ubiquitous phone shops around town, and pay-as-you-go cards (*'dianhua ka'*:

phone card) come in denominations of 50 or 100 yuan. Phone cards are available at most newsstands and small shops.

Another option is the International Post Office *(see Mail on page 87)*. Besides long-distance calls, it handles remittances, money orders and telegraphic money transfers.

Local telephone calls can be made from streetside booths with attendants, and also from many stores. Local calls usually cost 5 jiao. You will find that coin-operated phones are often out of order.

The country code for calling China is 86, and the area code for Beijing is 10.

Beijing has a large range of cheap Internet cafés with reasonably fast connections. Try 520 Digital Technology next to the Bainao Market south of Warker's Stadium, or wander through the Zhongguancun area.

Courier Services

Express courier services in Beijing include DHL (tel: 10-6466 5566), FedEx (tel: 10-6468 5566), TNT (tel: 800-810 9868) and UPS (tel: 10-6530 1234).

Media

The English-Language *China Daily* reports domestic and foreign news with an official slant. The *International Herald Tribune*, *Asian Wall Street Journal* and international news magazines are available at 5-star hotels

Most major hotels offer CNN's 24-hour programmes. Star TV from Hong Kong is also available. China Central Television broadcasts English-language news and programing on CCTV 9 while local programmes and most imported programmes are broadcast in Chinese. Local radio broadcasts in English and other languages can be heard on 91.5FM and 87.5FM.

USEFUL INFORMATION

Tourist Information and Websites

The Beijing Tourism Administration operates a hotline for emergencies and information, tel: 10-6513 0828. The English spoken at the other end is not always perfect, but if you need help or advice when you are away from your hotel, it is worth a try. Most hotels have their own travel desks for arranging hire cars and organised tours.

Make good use of the information desk or hotel concierge to check on events and opening and closing times of tourist sites. English-language publications listing ongoing events are available in restaurants, hotels and bars: *that's Beijing* is the leader; also avilable are *City Weekend*, *Beijing This Month* and *Time Out Beijing*.

Above: old post office, Dongliaominxian

For information on travelling elsewhere in China, contact your hotel's travel office, or China International Travel Service (CITS) (tel: 10-8522 8888; www.cits.com.cn). CITS is China's main state-run tourism bureau, which has branches throughout the country.

Useful websites sponsored by Beijing Tourism Administration and other government bodies include:

www.bta.gov.cn
www.chinatour.com
www.beijingtour.net.cn
www.cbw.com

Foreign Airline Offices

Air Canada: C201 Lufthansa Centre; tel: 10-6468 2001

Air France: Room 512 Fullliak Plaza; tel: 10-6588 1388

All Nippon Airways: 1/F Fa Zhan Tower, Dongshanhuan Beilu; tel: 10-6590 9191

Asiana Airlines: Room 102 Lufthansa Centre; tel: 10-6468 4000

British Airways: Room 210 Scitech Tower; tel: 10-8511 5599

Dragonair: Room 1710, Henderson Centre, 18 Jianguomennei Dajie; tel: 10-6518 2533

Finnair: Room 102 Scitech Tower; tel: 10-6512 7180

Japan Airlines: Hotel New Otani, Chang Fu Gong Office Building; tel: 10-6513 0888

KLM: Room 501 China World Trade Centre; tel: 10-6505 3505

Korean Air: Room 901 Hyundai Millenium Building, 38 Xiaoyun Lu; tel: 10-8453 8888

Lufthansa: S101 and C202 Beijing Lufthansa Centre; tel: 10-6465 4488

SAS: Room 1830, Sunflower Tower, Maizidian Lu; tel: 10-8527 6100

Singapore Airlines: 8/F Tower 2 China World Trade Centre; tel: 10-6505 2233

Swissair: 6/F Scitech Tower; tel: 10-6512 3555

United Airlines: 1/F Office Building Lufthansa Centre; tel: 10-6463 1111

Embassies

Australia: 21 Dongzhimen Wai Dajie; tel: 10-6532 2331; fax: 10-6532 4605

Canada: 19 Dongzhimen Wai Dajie; tel: 10-6532 3536; fax: 10-6532 4311

France: 3 Dongsan Jie, Sanlitun; tel: 10-6532 1331; fax: 10-6532 4841

Germany: 17 Dongzhimen Wai Dajie; tel: 10-6532 2161; fax: 10-6532 5336

Italy: 2 Dong'er Jie, Sanlitun; tel: 10-6532 2131; fax: 10-6532 4676

Japan: 7 Ritian Lu, Jianguomen Wai; tel: 10-6532 2361; fax: 10-6532 4625

Netherlands: 4 Lingmahe Nanlu; tel: 10-6532 1131; fax: 10-6532 4689

New Zealand: Dong'er Jie, Ritan Lu; tel: 10-6532 2731; fax: 10-6532 4317

Norway: 1 Dongyi Jie, Sanlitun; tel: 10-6532 2261; fax: 10-6532 2392

Russia: 4 Dongzhimenbei Zhongjie; tel: 10-6532 1267; fax: 10-6532 4851

Singapore: 1 Xiushui Beijie; tel: 10-6532 1115; fax: 10-6532 2215

South Korea: Dongsijie, Sanlitun; tel: 10-6532 0290; fax: 10-6532 0141

Spain: 9 Sanlitun Lu; tel: 10-6532 1986; fax: 10-6532 3401

Sweden: 3 Dongzhimen Wai Dajie; tel: 10-6532 9770; fax: 10-6532 5008

Switzerland: Dongwu Jie, Sanlitun; tel: 10-6532 2736; fax: 10-6532 4353

Thailand: 40 Guanghua Lu; tel: 10-6532 1749; fax: 10-6532 1748

UK: 11 Guanghua Lu; tel: 10-5192 4000; fax: 10-6532 1937

USA: 3 Xiushui Beijie; tel: 10-6532 3831; fax: 10-6532 5141

LANGUAGE

Large hotels usually have many English-speaking staff. Otherwise, you'll find that most people speak only a little English. English, French, Japanese, Italian, German and Spanish interpreters can be employed through major hotels or CITS. Prices are negotiable depending on the group's size.

Left: Beijing's new telephone booths

Useful Phrases

Hello/How are you?	ni hao
Goodbye	zai jian
Thank You	xie xie
I'm sorry/Excuse me	dui bu qi
No problem	mei (you) wen ti
How much does it cost?	duo shao qian?
Wait a moment	deng yi xia
No, don't have	mei you
It doesn't matter	mei (you) guan xi
I want	wo yao
Good	hao
Bad	bu hao
Not possible	bu xing
restaurant	fan dian
taxi	chu zu qi che
telephone	dian hua
hotel	bin guan
train	huo che
airplane	fei ji
restroom	ce suo
north	bei
south	nan
east	dong
west	xi
middle	zhong
street	jie
avenue	dajie
road	lu
gate	men
outside	wai
inside	nei
one	yi
two	er
three	san
four	si
five	wu
six	liu
seven	qi
eight	ba
nine	jiu
ten	shi

FURTHER READING

China Pop: How Soap Operas, Tabloids and Bestsellers Are Transforming a Culture. Zha Jianying. New Press, 1995. Zha takes an off-beat look at the explosion of Chinese popular culture in the 1980s and 1990s.

China Remembers by Zhang Lijia and Calum MacLeod. Oxford University Press, 1999. A fascinating and accessible look at New China through the eyes of 33 people who have vivid memories of five decades.

The Hermit of Peking by Hugh Trevor-Roper. This account of the life of alleged forger and Sinologist Edmund Backhouse is a marvellous piece of research by the late historian.

Hiking Around Beijing by Bennet, Seema, Mason, Pinnegar *et al*. Foreign Language Press, 2003. Put together by Beijing Hikers (www.beijinghikers.com), this book features maps and route details for day trips.

Hiking on History by William Lindesay. Oxford University Press, 2000. Indispensable for hikers, this is a guide to walking on several unrestored, less-visited sections of the Great Wall near Beijing.

In the Red, Geremie Barme. Columbia University Press, 1999. An academic examination of literary trends in China since 1989, especially the voices of dissent.

Insider's Guide to Beijing edited by Adam Pillsbury. Shantou University Press, 2004. Released by *that's Beijing*, this guide features in-depth information on everything, from the arts to doing business.

On a Chinese Screen by Somerset Maugham, Oxford University Press, 1997. Maugham, who first published this travelogue in 1922, wrote brief but engaging sketches of some of the local and foreign characters he met in Beijing.

Peking Opera by Colin MacKerras. Oxford University Press, 1997. A simple explanation of the history and standard forms of the art of Peking opera. Part of the Oxford Images of Asia series.

The Forbidden City: Centre of Imperial China (Discoveries) by Gilles Beguin and Dominique Morel. Abrams, 1997. A brief account details the daily lives of Ming and Qing emperors in the former imperial palace.

The Search for Modern China by Jonathan Spence. Norton, 1990. This brings to life Chinese society and politics over the past 400 years.

Wild Swans: Three Daughters of China by Jung Chang. Anchor Books, 1991. Adding plenty of historical detail, Wild Swans records 20th-century China through the lives of three generations of women, starting with the author's concubine grandmother.

Right: toffee apples for sale

ACKNOWLEDGEMENTS

Cover	**Zhang Zhenguang/Alamy**
Backcover	**Marcus Wilson Smith/APA**
Photography	**Marcus Wilson Smith/APA and**
Pages 76	**Bodo Bondzio**
32T	**Lance Dawning**
15, 30, 41T/B, 45T, 48T, 52T, 59, 61, 63T/B, 73, 77	**Kari Huus**
67	**Catherine Karnow**
6T, 11, 12, 13, 14, 16	**Manfred Morgenstern**
28	**Erhard Pansegrau**
10, 51, 68	**Photobank**
60	**Panos Pictures**
23	**Andrea Pistolesi**
49	**David Sanger**
62	**Peter Scheckmann**
52B	**Machtelb Stikvoort**
54	**Tom Till**
32B	**Elke Wandel**
74, 75	**Xinhua News Agency**
Cartography	**Maria Donnelly**
Cover Design	**Carlotta Junger**
Production	**Caroline Low**

© APA Publications GmbH & Co. Verlag KG Singapore Branch, Singapore

INDEX